THE HARVARD REVIEW OF PHILOSOPHY

φ

To make room for a steady flow of excellent submissions, we've distributed this year's content over two full-length issues: this issue focuses more on the philosophy of mind and moral philosophy, and the next one, due out early in 2005, focuses more on logic and the philosophy of language. But in keeping with our tradition of variety in subject matter, both contain papers and interviews on many areas of philosophy. Our tradition of philosophical dialogue continues as well; this issue starts with an exchange between John Foster and David Armstrong on perception and ends with an interview with John Searle, to whose criticisms Hubert Dreyfus responds in our next issue. All of our content, past and present, will soon be available for free on our website, www.harvardphilosophy.com, which also accepts orders for subscriptions and back issues.

 This year, like each of the last few, marks the passing of several philosophers of immense talent and influence. Bernard Williams was an amazing intellect and a personal inspiration to many of us at the *Review*, and we are honored to include in this volume an interview with him which, as far as we know, is the last one he gave. We will all miss him.

 Our warmest thanks go to all of the people who continue to support the *Review*. Our trustees—William Roberts, Joshua Harlan, Eric Henson, Stephen Mathes, and John Simkiss, Jr.—have kept our journal alive for so many years, and we could never have kept it going without them. We thank Thomas Scanlon and Alison Simmons for their advice and guidance, Mick Arellano and Sonia Sachs for excellent editorial assistance, and Nanette de Maine for helping us in more ways than we could possibly name. And, as always, we are grateful to the distinguished philosophers whose work fills this issue.

Eugene Chislenko and Benjamin Stoll

THE HARVARD REVIEW OF PHILOSOPHY
SPRING 2004 | VOLUME XII

EUGENE CHISLENKO   BENJAMIN STOLL
Editors-in-Chief

ZOË SACHS-ARELLANO
Managing Editor

NATHANIEL CRAIG, PAT SMITH, PETER EPSTEIN,
DANIEL LASSITER, KENNETH WALDEN
Senior Editors

DOUGLAS BEMIS, MICHAL DOUSA, BRAD DREW, ALEXANDER ELLIS,
ZACHARY HALE, ROLAND LAMB, DANIEL LING, ARI MOSKOWITZ,
AGNIESZKA RAFALSKA, JUSTIN SANTISTEVAN, CARL SCHOONOVER,
ANDY SILVER, JON WEISS, FRANK WHITE, DANIEL WILLIAMS
Editorial Staff

THE HARVARD REVIEW OF
PHILOSOPHY

VOLUME XII | SPRING 2004

Bernard Williams gives his last interview. **Page 81**

John Searle discusses his approach to philosophy. **Page 93**

The Problem of Perception

By John Foster

§1.   WHAT IS IT FOR SOMEONE TO PERCEIVE A PHYSICAL ITEM? I WANT TO PURSUE this question in the framework of physical realism—the framework of the assumption that the physical world is something whose existence is logically independent of the human mind and metaphysically fundamental. The choice of this common-sense framework might seem hardly worth mentioning. But, as will emerge, I have a special reason for doing so.

Within this realist framework, there are two rival general views of the nature of physical-item perception. One is what I shall call the *mediational view* (MV). This holds that whenever someone perceives a physical item, his perceptual contact with it is mediated by his being in some more fundamental psychological state. More precisely, it holds that whenever someone perceives a physical item, there is a certain psychological state (type-state) that is not in itself physical-item perceptive, such that his perceptual contact with that item breaks down into (is wholly constituted by) two components: one consists in his being in that state; the other comprises certain additional facts, but ones that do not involve anything further about his psychological condition at the relevant time. These additional facts will concern such things as the qualitative relationship of the psychological state to the physical item and the role of the item in the causing of the relevant realization of the state. The other position is what I shall call the *basic-relational view* (BV). This holds that whenever someone perceives a physical item, and when there is no other physical item which, in the context of that perception, he perceives more immediately, then his perceptual contact with that item is something psychologically basic. It does not, at the psychological level, break down into more fundamental factors; at least, it does not do so except (if this is possible) in a purely trivial way, when the perception

---

John Foster is a Fellow and Tutor in Philosophy at Brasenose College, Oxford. His main interests are in the fields of metaphysics, epistemology, and mind. He is well-known for his defence of unfashionable views, which include a Cartesian conception of the self, a sense-datum approach to the nature of perceptual experience, and an idealist account of the physical world. He has also proposed a new solution to the problem of induction, and, in his recent book The Divine Lawmaker, *has combined this with a new account of the nature of natural laws. His other books are:* The Case for Idealism, Ayer, The Immaterial Self, *and* The Nature of Perception.

of a complex item exhaustively decomposes into the separate perceptions of its parts.

These two views of the nature of perception are obviously mutually exclusive; at least, they are so on the assumption that we do sometimes perceive physical items. They are also, case by case, jointly exhaustive, in the sense that, taking any instance of physical-item perception, and focusing on the physical item that is most immediately perceived, we can see that the subject's perception of that item must either be psychologically basic in accordance with BV or break down into further factors in the way envisaged by MV. The problem, as I see it, is that neither view allows us to achieve, in any instance, a satisfactory account. The argument I shall present is one that I have developed in much greater detail in my book *The Nature of Perception;*[1] from time to time, I shall make reference to that more detailed discussion.

I shall start by considering the situation of BV, a position that can be thought of as a strong version of direct realism.

§2.   IT IS SOMETIMES THOUGHT THAT WE CAN DISPOSE OF BV QUITE QUICKLY, BY focusing on the case of hallucinatory experience and the kinds of way in which such experience can be induced.[2] Thus suppose, without his knowledge, scientists have attached a small radio-controlled device to someone's optic nerves, in a way that allows them to control, moment by moment, the pattern of their firings. Now imagine that, on successive days, the subject is sitting on the beach looking out to sea. On the first day, the device is switched off; a ship goes by, and, with his visual system working normally, the subject sees it. On the second day, there is no ship; but the device is activated to produce a pattern of firings just like that induced by the light from the ship on the earlier occasion, and these firings, in turn, produce an exactly similar response in the brain. As a result, the subject has a hallucinatory experience, as of seeing a ship, and we can plausibly suppose that this experience is subjectively indistinguishable from his perceptive experience of the previous day. Because, from the optic nerves onwards, the character of the neural process that occurs in the two cases is the same, it seems that we can reasonably assume that the character of the psychological outcomes will, at the fundamental level of description, be the same as well—the same not just in introspective appearance, but intrinsically. And since the psychological state involved in the hallucinatory case is not in itself perceptive, it would then follow that the psychological state fundamentally involved in the perceptive case is not in itself perceptive either. But if this latter state is not in itself perceptive, then the subject's perceptual contact with the ship, or with whatever physical item he most immediately perceives, cannot be, in the relevant sense, psychologically basic.[3] Rather, it must decompose into further factors in the way envisaged by MV. And if this is so for the case of the ship, it must presumably be so for physical-item perception quite generally.

This line of argument against BV seems, at first sight, to be a powerful one, and indeed I too once thought it decisive.[4] But I have now come to think that the basic-relationalist has an effective reply. Obviously, if he is to maintain his position, he has to insist that, while perception and hallucination may sometimes be subjectively indistinguishable, the psychological states that are fundamentally involved in them are always intrinsically different.[5] But I think that he has a way of doing this without embarrassment. For, in response to the fact that perception and hallucination can be preceded by neural processes of exactly the same kind, he can insist that the character of the immediately preceding process is not the only factor that is causally relevant to the character of the psychological outcome. Specifically, he can say that the character of the psychological outcome directly causally depends, in part, on the way in which this preceding neural process is itself brought about: in the particular case on which we are focusing, the way in which, on the first day, the firings in the optic nerves are brought about by the transmission of light from the ship combines with the resulting neural process to ensure the realization of a psychological state that is in itself perceptive, while the way in which, on the second day, the firings in the optic nerves are brought about by the use of the device combines with the resulting neural process to ensure the realization of a psychological state that is hallucinatory. The kinds of causal process here envisaged might seem strange when compared with the kinds of causal process we find in the physical realm. But when we take account of the special character of the psychological states which the basic-relationalist takes to be involved in perception—states that are inherently perceptive of particular physical items—the causation envisaged can, I think, be seen to be unproblematic: it can be seen to be precisely what the special character of these states calls for independently of the theorist's need to rebut the argument brought against him. This is not something that I have time to enlarge on in the present context, but I cover it in detail in my book.[6]

§3.   ALTHOUGH I THINK THAT THE BASIC-RELATIONALIST CAN HOLD HIS GROUND against the argument from hallucination, it seems to me that his position fails for a different reason.

Whenever a physical item is perceived, it is perceived under a certain sensible appearance—an appearance characterized by sensible qualities associated with the sense-realm in question. Thus when an item is seen, it is seen under a sensible appearance characterized by qualities of color and spatial, or spatiotemporal, arrangement, and when an item is heard, it is heard under a sensible appearance characterized by qualities of sound and temporal arrangement.[7] Now the sensible appearance of a physical item, though it is *of* something external, is *to* a perceiving mind. So whenever a physical item is perceived, there is something in the content of the perceptual experience that embodies the item's sensible appearance in its mental aspect—something that we might describe as the *way the subject is appeared to*. Let us refer to this element in the experience as its *phenomenal content*. Any theory of perception is obliged to give an account of the nature of this content and of its intimate relationship to perceptual contact.

What account, then, can the basic-relationalist give? Well, I think that the position to which he would be initially drawn, partly because of its simplicity, and partly because it is in line with how we ordinarily interpret our perceptual experiences in the course of everyday life, is what we might call the *presentational view*. According to this, perceiving works like a kind of mental spotlight, a beam of presentational awareness. In its mental substance, it is perfectly transparent, having no specific internal character or content beyond its being a perceptual awareness of a certain sense-modal (for example, visual or auditory) kind; and it acquires the whole of its phenomenal content by simply being directed onto, and thereby, as it were, presentationally illuminating in the relevant sense-modal way, a certain portion, or concrete aspect, of the physical environment. Of course, the exact form of the phenomenal content that this awareness acquires depends not just on its own modality and the sensible character of the item it presents, but also on the perspective in which this item is presented. The phenomenal content of the experience of seeing a round thing from an oblique angle is not the same as that of the experience of seeing it straight on, and the content involved in seeing something in the distance is different from that involved in seeing it close to. Obviously this is something which the presentationalist must take into account. He must claim that the phenomenal content draws its qualitative ingredients from the sensible character of the presented item in a form that is relativized to the relevant presentational perspective. This 'drawing' of the qualitative ingredients is, it must be stressed, an *ontological*, not just a *causal*, matter: it is not just that the presence of an item with a certain sensible character *causes* the subject to have a visual experience with a matching content; it is that the ingredients of the content are themselves the very elements of the external situation made experientially present. The featuring of a quality in the phenomenal content is not something ontologically separate from its external realization in the perceived item (something that merely serves to *represent* that realization), but is that realization itself brought immediately before the mind.

The presentational view is the position to which the basic-relationalist would be initially drawn. But, offered as a general theory, it is open to a decisive objection. For it cannot accommodate cases of *non-veridical* perception, where a physical item is perceived, but under a sensible appearance which misrepresents its true character. That such cases occur can hardly be denied—at least on the assumption that we perceive physical items at all. The notorious case of the stick partially immersed in water (in reality straight, but appearing bent) is an obvious example—though if it were thought (surely implausibly) that the presentationalist could handle this either by assimilating it to the case of seeing veridically but in a special perspective, or by claiming that what is immediately perceived is not the stick itself, but the light-array it transmits to the subject's eye, then we could switch our attention to such phenomena as astigmatism and color-blindness, where the distorting physical factors lie within the subject's own visual system. In whatever form they arise, the presentational view cannot accommodate cases of non-veridical perception because, in taking the qualitative ingredients of phenomenal content to be directly drawn from the external item, it excludes the possibility of the sensible appearance of this item being at variance with its true character. Sensible appearance just is, for the presentationalist, the direct bringing of the item's actual character, in the relevant perspective, before the subject's mind.

Although the presentational view cannot deal with cases of non-veridical perception, and so cannot be accepted as a general theory about phenomenal content, there is still the option of retaining it for cases of veridical perception. So, in the case where a straight stick in water looks bent, we are forced to say that the featuring of bentness in the phenomenal content is not the featuring of some physical instance of bentness. But, in the case where a straight stick out of water looks (veridically) straight, we could still say that the featuring of straightness in the phenomenal content consists in the instance of straightness in the stick being made present to the mind. But while this mixture of approaches is an option, it is hardly a plausible one. For it is very hard to suppose that the veridicality or non-veridicality of an experience correlates with such a fundamental difference in its nature. Given that the sort of veridical and non-veridical experiences we are envisaging are alike in being physically perceptive, and that they causally originate from the perceived physical items by processes of a broadly similar kind, there is strong pressure to think of them as amenable to a unitary account. This pressure becomes, to my mind, irresistible when we focus on a case where a shift from veridical to non-veridical perception involves only very slight changes to the qualitative character of the phenomenal content and to the details of the causal process from the relevant physical item. Think, for example, of a situation in which someone first looks at an object through plain flat glass, seeing its shape as it is, and then looks at it through glass whose very slight degree of curvature imposes a correspondingly slight distortion on the way the shape of the object appears. It would surely be absurd to deny that these two perceptive experiences are, in their intrinsic character, of the same generic type.

Granted that he needs a unitary account of veridical and non-veridical perception, the basic-relationalist is obliged to conclude that, in all cases of perception, the qualitative ingredients of phenomenal content are wholly internal to the mind, rather than ontologically drawn from the physical items perceived. Let us speak of this position as the *internalist view*. Note that this view is to be taken as (exclusively) a version of BV: it combines the relevant claim of internality with the claim that perceptual contact with the relevant external item is psychologically basic.

The internalist view avoids the problem for the presentationalist: since the ingredients of phenomenal content are not ontologically drawn from the perceived item, there is no difficulty in understanding how phenomenal content can be at variance with the item's true character. But it faces problems of a different kind.

The basic problem is that it is hard to see how, on the internalist view, phenomenal content and perceptual contact fit together. There is no difficulty, in this respect, for the presentationalist: as he sees it, phenomenal content is precisely what perceptual contact automatically supplies by virtue of its presentational character—by the way in which it directly brings before the mind certain qualitative aspects of the external environment. Likewise, there is no difficulty here for the mediationalist: as he sees it, phenomenal content is the most crucial component of the mediating psychological state, and so is one of the factors that constitutively contributes to the securing of perceptual contact. The difficulty is in seeing what other option is available—what might explain how the content can embody the sensible appearance under which the item is perceived without being linked to the perceiving in either a presentational or a mediational way. It seems that, without such a link, phenomenal content will turn out to be, at best, an experiential accompaniment of perception, rather than something genuinely involved in it. And, of course, without a suitably involved content, it becomes impossible to think of the relation itself, between subject and item, as genuinely perceptual. Maybe the internalist will try to explain the involvement of content in contact in adverbial terms: perhaps he will say that phenomenal content is the experiential *mode* of perceiving, the experiential *manner* in which perceptual contact is achieved. But this is just the *schema* for an account: it does not tell us how, if not in a presentational or a mediational way, it is possible for there to be such a mode of perceiving.

One specific way in which this basic problem manifests itself is with respect to what I shall speak of as the *appropriateness requirement*. What I mean by this is the fact that, in order for a perceptual experience to be a genuine perception of some physical item, or, more precisely, to be a genuine perception which is not mediated by the perception of some other physical item, its phenomenal content has to be, to an adequate degree, qualitatively appropriate to that item. The best way to see this is to focus on a case where all the other conditions associated with perception are present, but the factor of appropriateness is conspicuously absent. Thus suppose I am in my sitting room, with my eyes turned towards the clock on the mantelpiece, with nothing obstructing my line of vision, and with all the other external factors favoring the achievement of visual contact. And suppose that light reflected from the clock and its surroundings enters my eyes in the normal way and sets up the appropriate kind of process in my optic nerves, which in turn transmits the appropriate signals to my brain. But then something peculiar happens. My brain responds to the incoming signals in a totally bizarre way, producing a visual experience which is not remotely like the sort of experience that is normal for that kind of photic input. It might be that the resulting experience is like that of seeing something quite different, such as a football match, or it might be that its content is not amenable to interpretation in ordinary terms at all. Now it is surely clear that, given the extent of the disparity between the real character of the external environment and the content of my experience, this experience is not physically perceptive. It is true that the clock and its surroundings play a causal role in producing the experience, and, with respect to the photic input, this role is of the normal kind for the circumstances in question. And we can even suppose that, as in the case of normal visual perception, the brain response preserves a kind of causal isomorphism between elements of the resulting experience and elements of the input, so that, relative to a suitably fine-grained division, different elements of the experience causally trace back to different elements of the relevant portion of the environment. But it would be absurd to suppose that the experience qualifies as an actual seeing of this portion, and that the only way in which its deviant content affects the situation is in making this seeing radically non-veridical. It is just as obvious that, in the context of the conditions envisaged, the extent of the non-veridicality precludes visual contact altogether. So here we have a clear illustration of the point at issue, that perceptual contact with the physical world requires an adequate degree of qualitative appropriateness of the phenomenal content of the perceptual experience to the physical item perceived. A point I should here mention is that, once we have rejected the presentational view, we should not think of appropriateness as entirely a matter of veridicality. For it will be partly a matter of conformity to what is normal, or normative, for the conditions of observation in question (so that, for example, the appropriate way of seeing a straight stick in water is as bent). But the precise conditions for appropriateness is not something that we need here pursue.

It is undeniable that the appropriateness requirement holds. But it creates difficulties for the internalist in two ways.

In the first place, the internalist does not seem to have any way of accounting for it. Considering the issue of explanation in the abstract, we can see two clear-cut ways in which someone could try to explain why the requirement holds. On the one hand, there is the explanation offered by the mediationalist. He would say that a sufficient degree of appropriateness is a *constitutive element* of perceptual contact: an experience that is perceptive is so partly *in virtue of* the way in which, relative to perspective, its phenomenal content is, to the relevant degree, representationally appropriate to the external item in question. On the other hand, there is the explanation offered by the presentationalist. According to him, perception just is, in perspective, the transparent displaying of the item's sensible character: there is no room for any degree of inappropriateness (which, for the presentationalist, would be the same as non-veridicality), since it is only in so far as it is drawn from the actual qualities of the perceived item that there is phenomenal content at all. Both these accounts of perception, would, in their contrasting ways, provide a complete rationale for the appropriateness requirement. But neither of them, of course, is available to the internalist. Nor, as far as I can see, can he derive a rationale from any other source: in rejecting both the presentational and mediational accounts, he leaves himself without resources for explaining why there is any limit on the degree of inappropriateness that perception can tolerate.

The second point involves something more subtle. Although there is a limit on the degree of inappropriateness which physical-item perception can tolerate, there is surely no objective answer to the question of precisely where, in any specific type of case, this limit falls. Its precise location is surely, rather, a matter for decision; or at least, this is surely what we must accept once we have rejected a full-blooded presentational view, which excludes inappropriateness altogether. Thus suppose we have a device which can be used to distort the visual appearance of the physical scene by sending a stream of radiation through the subject's visual cortex, the degree of the distortion increasing with the strength of the radiation. And let us suppose that we are currently using this device on someone who is looking at an apple. At one extreme, with very weak radiation, we can envisage an effect on phenomenal content so slight that there is no threat to the continuation of visual contact: the subject continues to see the apple, but perhaps its apparent shape is a little warped or its surface color pattern looks blurred. At the other extreme, with very strong radiation, we can envisage an effect so great that visual contact is clearly severed: how things appear to the subject bears no resemblance at all to how things are, and the experience cannot, by any stretch of the imagination, be construed as perceptive. But, between these extremes, we can also, surely, envisage a range of cases that are inherently borderline — cases whose classification as perceptive or hallucinatory is a matter for stipulation rather than a question of objective fact. To reach such cases, we need only envisage a series, from the one extreme to the other, in which we very gradually increase the strength of the radiation and the consequent degree of effect on the subject's experience. It seems clear that, somewhere in the middle, we shall come upon cases where the question of whether the extent of the inappropriateness is sufficiently great to sever visual contact with the apple has no definite answer, even from a God's-eye view.

The existence of these borderline cases is easy enough to explain in the framework of MV, which takes a subject's perceptual contact with a physical item to be partly constituted by the fact that his experience stands in the right sort of qualitative relationship to it. For the borderline cases will then arise in this area in the way that they do in any area where, holding constant other relevant factors, the application of a concept wholly depends on whether the situation achieves a sufficient value along a certain qualitative dimension, but where there is no particular point on this dimension that marks a theoretically critical division. Thus the existence of the borderline cases would be explained in the same sort of way as we explain why there is sometimes no objective answer to the question of whether some group of people is sufficiently numerous to count as a "crowd" or the question of whether someone has enough hair on his head to avoid counting as "bald." But the situation of the internalist is quite different. For even if he could find some rationale for the appropriateness requirement itself, his commitment to BV would prevent him from explaining, or even acknowledging, such borderline cases. After all, perceptual contact itself, unlike qualitative appropriateness, does not admit of degrees: it is all or nothing. So if such contact is taken to be psychologically basic—something which does not, at the psychological level, break down into more fundamental factors— there is nothing at the psychological level of description which could explain how the question of its obtaining could ever fail to have an objective and fully determinate answer.

In the light of all this, it seems to me that the internalist view cannot provide an adequate account of the relationship between phenomenal content and perceptual contact. And since the presentational view has also proved unsatisfactory, and there are no other options available to the basic-relationalist, I conclude that BV itself must be rejected, and rejected for all cases of perception.

§4.   WITH THE REJECTION OF THE BASIC-RELATIONAL VIEW, LET US NOW TURN TO the alternative account of perception offered by the mediational view (MV). This claims that whenever someone perceives a physical item, his perceptual contact with it is mediated by his being in some more fundamental psychological state. More precisely, it claims that this contact breaks down into two components, one of which consists in his being in a certain, not in itself physically perceptive, psychological state, and the other of which comprises certain additional facts, but ones that do not involve anything further about the subject's psychological condition at the relevant time. These additional facts concern such things as the qualitative relationship of the psychological state to the relevant physical item and the role of the item in the causing of the relevant realization of the state.

Since we have rejected BV for all cases of perception, it seems that we have no choice but to embrace MV. But the trouble is that MV too seems vulnerable to a crucial objection. For it seems that the sort of relationship which it envisages between the subject and the relevant external item would not qualify as one of genuine perceiving at all. The problem is disarmingly simple. Perceiving is, by definition, a form of awareness: to perceive something is to be perceptually aware of it. But in the situation envisaged, where the only psychological state fundamentally involved is not in itself physically perceptive, it seems that the subject's awareness never reaches beyond the boundaries of his own mind. For how can the relevant additional factors, which do not involve anything further about the subject's current psychological condition, turn the not-in-itself-physically-perceptive state into an awareness of something external? How can they create a genuine awareness of the relevant physical item if they only concern such things as the way in which this item qualitatively relates to the psychological state and the role it plays in causing the subject to come into this state?

This point is most familiar, and seems especially clear, in the case where MV is developed along its traditional empiricist lines—the empiricist tradition of Locke, Hume, Russell, and Ayer—in which the core of the relevant psychological state is held to consist in the occurrence of a mental object of awareness: the sensory idea or sense-impression or sense-datum. For it then seems quite evident that, even if they serve to *represent* things in the external environment, these mental items are the only things of which we are genuinely perceptually aware; and if it were not for the fact that we come to interpret these items as external (an interpretation induced by the world-suggestive character of their organization), we would never even think of our awareness as reaching to anything beyond the contents of our own minds. The point is sometimes metaphorically expressed by saying that, on the traditional empiricist account, the mental objects of awareness form a kind 'veil of perception', which blocks our access to the external things that lie beyond.

In the cases where the mediating psychological state does not involve the occurrence of a mental object of awareness—as when, for example, the mediationalist adopts some form of cognitive account[8] or adverbial theory[9]—the problem is less conspicuous but still there. There is now no rival class of perceptual objects to form a metaphorical veil— a barrier at which the reach of perceptual awareness can be seen to terminate. But given that the only psychological states fundamentally involved are not in themselves physically perceptive, it still seems that there will be no genuine awareness of the external environment, and that, at best, the relevant states will enable the subject to gain information about it. For it still seems that if these states do not, on their own, suffice to give the subject a genuine awareness of something external, then there is no way in which factors that do not add anything to his psychological condition could make up the deficiency. I might add, in passing, that versions of MV that do not postulate mental objects of awareness are also, in my view, unsatisfactory for a different reason, since they fail to do justice to the phenomenological character of perceptual experience. Specifically, I think that, without the postulation of these internal sensory objects, the mediationalist cannot explain why it experientially seems to the subject that there is something of which he is perceptually, and in particular presentationally, aware. Once again, this is a point that I cover in detail in my book.[10]

The *prima facie* objection to MV, then, is that, even if our relationship to the physical items we suppose ourselves to perceive is mediated in the way it envisages, this relationship does not meet the requirements of genuine perception, since it does not allow our awareness to reach beyond the boundaries of our own minds. I can see only one way in which the mediationalist could try to rebut this objection. In our ordinary thinking, we seem to recognize various types of case in which the perceiving of one physical item is in some way mediated by the perceiving of another. For example, we are happy to accept that someone can watch a football match on television, when we know that his visual access to the match is channelled through his access to the patterns on the screen. Likewise, we are happy to speak of a radar operator as seeing an approaching missile, when we know that his only way of detecting it is by seeing some signal on his monitor. Or again, we think nothing of saying that we can hear the approach of an ambulance when the only indicator of its presence is the sound of its siren. Even with respect to cases that we take to be paradigmatically perceptive, it is often obvious that the subject's contact with the object in question is achieved through his contact with one of its parts. So, by all ordinary standards, I now have a clear view of the apple on the table in front of me; but obviously I only have this view of the apple by virtue of seeing a certain portion of its surface. All these seem to be cases where we ordinarily recognize the subject's perceptual contact with one physical item as mediated by his contact with another. This might be thought to indicate that our actual concept of perception is sufficiently flexible to tolerate an MV account after all. Indeed, it might be thought to show that MV cannot even be excluded when it is developed in its traditional empiricist way, where the problem for the mediationalist had seemed especially clear. For what is crucially different between a case of perceiving one physical item by perceiving another and perceiving a physical item by perceiving, or being aware of, a sensory item in the mind? It is to this supposed point of analogy that the mediationalist might appeal.

On casual inspection, such an appeal seems to offer some hope for the mediationalist, but it is a hope that evaporates when we examine the supposedly analogous cases in more detail. What we find, when we do, is that, in each instance, there is some factor that prevents the case from lending any support to MV.

Take first the case of someone following a football match on television. There is no denying that we ordinarily think of such a subject as able to see events on the football pitch, and we also recognize that his visual access to these events is in some way mediated by his visual access to what takes place on the screen. But, in order for this to help the cause of MV, the mediation in question has to be, like that postulated by MV itself, of a decompositional kind: it has to be such that, whenever the viewer makes perceptual contact with events on the pitch, this contact breaks down into (is wholly constituted by) his contact with events on the screen, together with certain other facts. It is here that things start to go wrong. It is true that there is a way of representing the mediation as decompositional. Thus we could claim, and indeed with some plausibility, that what is ultimately going on psychologically is that the subject visually registers patterns on the screen, but sees them—

experientially interprets them—as scenes from the match. And once this claim is accepted, it will be hard to deny that such contact as the subject has with the match ultimately breaks down into this registering and experiential interpreting, together with the causal process from the stadium to the television. But the trouble with this, as a potential source of support for MV, is that, once we have represented the mediation in these decompositional terms, it is no longer plausible to suppose that what is mediated is genuine perception. For the same considerations that seemed to show that, on the traditional empiricist version of MV, our perceptual awareness does not reach beyond the sensory items in the mind, would now lead us to say that the television viewer's perceptual awareness does not reach beyond the patterns on the screen. The only way we can plausibly think of the viewer as genuinely seeing the match is by taking his visual contact with it to be psychologically basic, and construing the mediational role of his access to the screen as merely causal—as consisting in the fact that his reception of light from the screen is an essential part of the causal process by which events on the pitch become visible to him. This would accord with how things experientially seem to the viewer himself, and, because of our own first-person familiarity with the televisual experience, it is how we tend to understand the situation in our ordinary thinking. But thus construed, the television case would obviously not provide an analogy for what is envisaged by MV, since the envisaged mediation would not be of the analogically relevant kind.

The case of the radar operator is equally of no help to the advocate of MV. There is no denying that such contact as the operator has with the missile is mediated by his perception of the signal on the screen and that this mediation is of a decompositional kind: the contact breaks down into the perception and recognition of the signal, and the causal link between the signal and the missile itself. And, in this case, unlike that of the television viewer, we are not, even in our ordinary thinking, inclined to understand the situation in any other way, since there is nothing in the phenomenology of the radar-monitoring experience that might tempt us to a different conclusion. But the trouble, once again, is that, once we take account of the decompositional nature of the situation, we are prevented from thinking of the contact with the missile as genuinely perceptual. Indeed, even in our ordinary thinking, we recognize it as obvious that the operator does not really see the missile, but merely detects its presence by inference from the signal. If, in ordinary usage, we are happy to speak of him as seeing the missile, this is only because ordinary usage does not aim to describe things as they strictly are. All these points also apply, *mutatis mutandis*, to the case of the ambulance and the siren.

There remains the case of perceiving a whole object by perceiving a part; and, at first sight, this may seem to be the ideal case for the defender of MV. On the one hand, there is no disputing the claim that the contact with the whole item is decompositionally mediated by contact with the part. Thus, whatever visual contact I can be said to have with the apple on the table in front of me, it is obvious that it breaks down into my contact with the relevant portion of its surface and the fact that this latter item *is* a portion of the apple's surface. On the other hand, the decompositional nature of the situation does not, in this case, make it difficult to accept that the contact with the whole object is genuinely perceptual. There is no temptation to say that, because all that is immediately visible to me is a certain portion of its surface, I do not really see the apple itself. On the face of it, then, we have here exactly the right sort of case for mediationalist's purposes—a case in which there is genuine perception combined with decompositional mediation. But, on reflection, I think we can see that the case could not be less helpful to his cause. For what here allows us to recognize the combination of genuine perception and decompositional mediation is that the two putative perceptual objects involved are not, as in the other cases we have considered, ontologically separate, and so are not thought of as competitors for the title of being what the subject really perceives. There is no difficulty in understanding how, in seeing a certain portion of its surface, I am seeing the apple itself, since contact with this portion just is contact with the apple in a locationally focused form. This cannot provide any analogical support for the mediational claims of MV. Even when MV is developed along its traditional empiricist lines, where the mediating psychological state involves an object of awareness, this object is located in the mind, not in the external world, and so has to be, on a grand scale, ontologically separate from the physical item supposedly perceived.

I have considered three types of case where it might be thought that the perceiving of one physical item is mediated by the perceiving of another, and none of them provides any analogical support for MV. In the case of the television viewer, the only way we can think of the subject as genuinely perceiving the football match is by taking the mediating role of his access to the screen to be merely causal. In the cases of the radar operator and the ambulance, there is no denying that the mediation involved is decompositional, but there is equally no question of thinking of the contact with the more remote item as genuinely perceptual. Finally, in cases like that of the apple, we must accept that there is both genuine perception and decompositional mediation, but, unlike anything that might be envisaged under MV, the two perceptual objects involved are not ontologically separate. Although there are other types of case that could be considered, I cannot think of any that would not fail, as something that might help the cause of MV, in one of these three ways, where either the relevant mediation is not decompositional, or the supposed remote perceptual object is not genuinely perceived, or the two perceptual objects are not ontologically separate; and, in consequence, I think that the appeal to the supposed analogy is unsuccessful.

With the failure of this analogical appeal, the original objection to MV stands, and I can see no further way in which it might be resisted. Our relationship to the physical items we think we perceive may well be as MV characterizes it; indeed, it seems that it *has* to be so if BV stands discredited. But if it is, then this relationship does not meet the requirements of genuine perception, since it does not allow perceptual awareness to reach beyond the boundaries of the mind.

§5.   IF MY ARGUMENTS HAVE BEEN RIGHT, THEN NEITHER BV NOR MV ALLOWS US to achieve a satisfactory account of physical-item perception. The problem with BV is that we simply do not have the kind of psychologically basic contact with physical items that it envisages; indeed, if there is to be provision for non-veridical perception, the kind of contact it envisages seems to be impossible. The problem with MV is that, while it is plausible to take our contact with physical items to be mediated in the way it envisages, such contact does not qualify as genuinely perceptual. Granted that BV and MV are, case by case, jointly exhaustive, we seem to be forced to the conclusion that we do not perceive physical items at all. This is a hugely unpalatable conclusion, not merely because of its affront to common sense, but also because all our beliefs about the physical world are founded on the assumption that perceptual access to the world is available.

As I see it, the only way in which we can hope to avoid this unwanted conclusion, and the epistemological havoc it would wreak, is by dropping the assumption of physical realism on which our whole discussion has so far been based. For, without this assumption, we would be free to embrace an idealist account of the physical world, and such an account, suitably developed, would allow us to eliminate the problem of perception at a stroke. Thus if we were to construe the world as something which is logically created by (or perhaps by something whose central component consists in) facts about human sense-experience — in particular by the physically thematic ways in which our sense-experiences are organized — we would no longer need to think of perceptual awareness as having to reach beyond the boundaries of the mind to make contact with the physical items themselves. The occurrence of a sensory experience could qualify as the perceiving of a physical item simply by virtue of its fitting into the overall organization of such experiences in the appropriate way.

The fact that idealism is the only position which allows for physical-item perception does not, of course, establish its truth; and there is no denying that it, in turn, faces a number of *prima facie* problems. Even so, the difficulty of accepting that we have no perceptual access to the physical world should at least lead us to give serious consideration to the idealist option. I have set out elsewhere the further steps by which I think that an idealist account of an appropriate kind can, in the end, be fully vindicated.[11] φ

Notes

[1] Oxford: Oxford University Press, 2000.

[2] See, in particular, H. Robinson, "The General Form of the Argument for Berkeleian Idealism" in ed. J. Foster and H. Robinson, *Essays on Berkeley* (Oxford: Oxford University Press, 1985), 170-7. And *Perception* (London: Routledge, 1994), 151-62.

[3] At each time over the relevant period, what the subject *immediately* perceives will be some slightly earlier time-slice of a certain portion of the ship's surface.

[4] Thus see my *Ayer* (London: Routledge & Kegan Paul, 1985), 147-9, 161.

[5] In other words, he has to accept what is known as a *disjunctive* account, in line with the proposal of J. Hinton in his *Experiences* (Oxford: Oxford University Press, 1973). Other advocates of this account have included P. Snowdon, "Perception, Vision, and Causation," *Proceedings of the Aristotelian Society* vol. 81 (1980-1): 175-92, and J. McDowell, "Criteria, Defeasibility, and Knowledge," *Proceedings of the British Academy*, vol. 68 (1982): 455-79.

[6] See my *The Nature of Perception*, pp. 23-43.

[7] Not all forms of appearance count as sensible in the relevant sense. For example, a path's looking dangerous or a preacher's sounding pompous are not sensible in this sense. For an account of what is distinctive about sensible appearance, see my *The Nature of Perception*, pp. 44-51.

[8] For example, see D. Armstrong, *A Materialist Theory of the Mind* (London: Routledge & Kegan Paul, 1968), ch. 10, and G. Pitcher, *A Theory of Perception* (Princeton: Princeton University Press, 1971).

[9] For example, see C. Ducasse, "Moore's Refutation of Idealism," in ed. P. Schilpp, *The Philosophy of G. E. Moore* (Chicago: Northwestern University Press, 1942), 223-51, and R. Chisholm, *Perceiving* (Ithaca: Cornell University Press, 1957), 115-25.

[10] In my *The Nature of Perception*, Part Three.

[11] In my *The Case for Idealism* (London: Routledge & Kegan Paul, 1982), and "The Succinct Case for Idealism," in ed. H. Robinson, *Objections to Physicalism* (Oxford: Oxford University Press, 1993), and my *The Nature of Perception*, Part Five.

In Defence of the Cognitivist Theory of Perception

By D. M. Armstrong

JOHN FOSTER'S BOOK, THE NATURE OF PERCEPTION (FOSTER, 2000), IS WRITTEN TO defend his Idealist, or Berkeleyan, theory of perception. One view that he is concerned to reject is what he usefully calls the 'Cognitivist' theory of perception. I am named as one of its defenders. His critique of the theory serves me as a good starting point and as a stimulus for a new defence of the theory.

In work done a long time ago (Armstrong, 1961 and 1968, Chapters 10 and 11) I argued that the central cases, at least, of perception are nothing more than acquirings of beliefs, beliefs about the current state of our environment. The environment here should be understood to include our own body, and elsewhere (Armstrong 1962 and 1968, Chapter 14) I argued that bodily sensations are to be understood as bodily perceptions. In Chapter 15 of the 1968 book I went on to argue for the 'inner sense' account of introspective awareness—consciousness in the most important sense of that difficult concept. Perception, bodily sensation and introspection were all to be thought of as, fundamentally, nothing but the acquiring of beliefs about the current state of our environment, our body, and our mind. The 'acquiring' part, by the way, I think I got from Gilbert Ryle, although I cannot trace a source. The important thing, of course, is what it is that is acquired. But that perception is an *event* of acquiring is, I think, a most useful insight.

Over the years I have not abandoned a theory of this sort, but I have been made to suffer for, and have regretted my using of, the word "belief" in articulating the theory. The problem is that belief is, it seems, such a sophisticated notion. It is natural to think that only a rather superior sort of mind, perhaps only the sort found in human beings, is capable of such a high-class act as believing things. But perception occurs

D.M. Armstrong was Challis Professor of Philosophy at the University of Sydney from 1964 to 1991; he is now Emeritus Professor of Philosophy at that university. He has held a great many visiting appointments at U.S. universities and colleges. Perhaps his best known book is A Materialist Theory of the Mind. *For the last twenty-five years he has concentrated on metaphysics, and his ontological views were set out in* A World of States of Affairs. *In May 2004 he delivered the Pufendorf Lectures at Lund University in Sweden. His most recent book is* Truth and Truthmakers.

in very low-class organisms indeed. Do evolutionarily primitive insects that can perceive have *beliefs*? It is hard to believe!

That is why I think John Foster's 'Cognitivist' is a much superior term. I myself have tried to weasel away from the word "belief" in a couple of ways. I regularly use the word "information" these days, as does Foster, in discussing the theory. That already sounds rather better, suggesting as it does information theory, whose key concept is reduction of uncertainty. But that concept may be suspected of being too wide, and in any case it is clear that information in the context of perception will have to cover *misinformation*. Non-veridical perception is still perception.

Something else that may sound rather bad at first hearing, but may actually be more helpful in articulating the cognitive theory, is another idea which I have also put to myself at times: that what is acquired in perception is a *propositional* state. What I mean by this is, of course, nothing linguistic. The idea is that the mental state involved has a structure with a certain complexity. It involves the attributing of a property to an object, or attributing the holding of a relation between two or more objects.

By contrast, non-cognitivist theories of perception have what one might call a '*thing* model' for perception. Perception is conceived of as a two-term relation between a mind and an object. Because of the need of any theory of perception to give an account of perceptual illusion, thing models rather naturally lead to the postulation of sense-data. A.J. Ayer's clever description of sense-data as 'junior substances' captures exactly their thing-like nature.

But returning to the propositional theory, the object or objects to which properties and relations are attributed are picked out indexically. Perception is concerned with the perceiver's body and its environment in the here and now, where the here and now is given by the place and date of the perception itself. It seems, however, not essential that the indexical component be represented within the perceptual structure. That would be much too sophisticated. But take the case where the perceiver *acts* on the basis of the perception. It is clear that the action *presupposes*, as it were, that the perceived structure of the body and environment is the particular structure that it putatively has at the time and place of the perception. Consider a device that is at a varying temperature, and whose output is a measurement not of absolute temperature but of the *difference* between its temperature and the temperature of its environment. There is something indexical in its output, which may cause the device to take certain action—action designed, say, to minimize the difference. But the non-relative temperature of the device is not represented in the output. The indexical character of perception need be no more than that found in the device.

In perception, properties and relations are attributed to objects. But the structure in the mind that is acquired when we perceive will not literally have these properties and relations. So there will have to be mere *representations* of sensible properties and relations in the structure.

This leads me to say that perception involves the employment of *concepts*, concepts of these properties and relations. (Of course, there will be individual concepts also in the structure of perceptions, but let us pass that complication by.) Since most perceivers are quite incapable of language, this means that we ought, given a Cognitivist theory of perception, to accept the reality of *non-linguistic* concepts. If this conclusion is resisted, then I am prepared to compromise and say instead that what a perceiver must have, and what figure in perceptual structures, are *discriminative capacities*. Each perceptual representation of a property or a relation involves a discriminative capacity, a capacity to discriminate (in behavior, as I take it) between an object's having, or lacking, the property or relation in question. (Not an infallible capacity, of course.) This logical tying of the perception of sensible qualities and relations to *action* is very important and seems essential if the problem of marking off perceptions from other mental activities such as imagings is to be achieved.

It may be noted that the status of the sensible qualities and relations is somewhat ambiguous. They belong to what Wilfrid Sellars called, in his great figure, the manifest image of the world. Some of us would want to go with Sellars and devalue these properties by comparison with the true, or at least truer, properties of the scientific image of the world as it is painfully articulated. I think that the sensible properties can still be accepted as real properties, even if "second-rate" properties, that is, properties that fail to carve nature at its true joints. It is true that our empirical knowledge begins with perception, and that perception, and therefore the manifest image, is the ultimate court of appeal in the testing of the theories embodied in the scientific image. Nevertheless, the scientific image works away from the manifest image at a number of points. In particular, a critique and a purging have to be conducted against the properties and relations found in the manifest image. I cannot, of course, defend that position in any depth here.

Various points now arise. Consider again this propositional structure of concepts or discriminative capacities. The structure attributes something to the world—a certain state of affairs, I am inclined to say. The attribution may be veridical or non-veridical. This last remark should make it clear that the mental states involved are *intentional* states, in the technical sense of the mediaevals that contemporary analytic philosophy has, to its great benefit, reacquainted itself with. The major mark of an intentional object is that there may or may not be a really existing object corresponding to it. I may add that I was brought to see this point by Elizabeth Anscombe's fine paper on the intentionality of sensation (Anscombe, 1965).

It may be objected that the introduction of intentionality once again threatens to sophisticate perception in an unacceptable manner. This, however, seems to be incorrect. Recent investigations have shown that the notion of intentionality may well admit of *degrees* of intentionality. The very lowest degree is to be found in purely physical objects, and is linked to their dispositions and powers. See in particular (Martin and Pfeifer, 1986). The late George Molnar went so far as to speak of *physical intentionality* in connection with dispositions and powers (Molnar, 2003). The 'intentionality' here is given by the fact that the dispositions and powers of particulars point, as it were, to *manifestations* of these dispositions and powers in suitable circumstances, yet the manifestations need never occur. More and more sophisticated intentionalities can be found in the goal-seeking and feedback mechanisms that are to be found in the organic world. It can then be seen that to give an account in terms of intentionalities does not over-sophisticate perception.

One thing that a propositional account finds easy to accept is the possibility of unconscious perception. Why should we not acquire cognitive structures of a certain sort that represent (or sometimes misrepresent) certain features of the current state of our body and its environment yet be introspectively unaware of what is thus acquired? Indeed, since introspective awareness is presumably the privilege of relatively few of the perceivers that the animal kingdom contains, should we not expect unconscious perception to be the norm? And in any case a great deal of scientific evidence now exists to show that unconscious perception occurs in human beings.

A matter that considerably exercises John Foster, and that he thinks is a difficulty for Cognitivist theory, is that of marking off perception from the having of mental images. Imaging is often involved in the memory of events, but can be the mere having of images. There is no doubt, as Berkeley and Hume in particular made clear, that perceiving and imaging resemble each other closely. And if the Cognitivist theory of perception is correct, then it is also clear that imaging will have to involve some sort of second-hand mobilization of the very same concepts—or discriminative capacities—that are found in perception. But, at the same time, Berkeley, Hume, and others have not had great success in marking off perception from imaging. As I have already said, the special link that perception has to current action, a link lacking in imaging, is very important and close to the essence of perception. But if we try to make the link to action part of a strict definition, counter-instances are rather easily produced.

I don't think that this problem is too important. It does seem important if you think that the problem has to be solved purely by philosophers using the method of conceptual analysis. It then becomes a very difficult problem that nobody has been able to solve. All the suggested conceptual marks have embarrassing counter-instances. But I suggest that the problem should not be thought of in this way. We should look to psychology and neurology for the exact account of the difference. We can start from the position that we have a perfectly good, unselfconscious grasp of what perception is—seeing, hearing, touching, tasting, and so forth—and its difference from mere imaging in these same modes. We might say, as Hume said of belief when he found himself unable to give any satisfactory definition of it (*Treatise*, Book I, Part III, Section VII), "its true and proper name is *perception*." Of imaging we can say "its true and proper description is the having of mental images." But the exact difference between perceiving and imaging remains to be spelled out by science, and not by us philosophers.

But now we must consider the traditional objection to cognitive theories of perception, one quite rightly insisted upon by Foster. As we all know, it is perfectly possible to have a perception that is in some respect non-veridical and yet not to attribute, or even have any inclination to attribute, the intentional content of the perception to reality. The straight stick or oar that looks half bent when the lower end is placed in water is a traditional example. We may be perfectly familiar with the phenomenon, accept that the objects look bent, but not *attribute* bentness to them. This case not only constitutes a difficulty for cognitivism in perception, but also casts some doubt upon the alleged link between perception and action. There is, of course, a true counterfactual involved. We have *independent* good reasons, aside from the perception, for thinking that the objects are really straight. If we did not have these reasons, then we would have attributed bentness in such cases. Nevertheless, there is no actual attribution.

This objection used to trouble me a good deal. But now I do not think that it is really too serious. The propositional gloss on the cognitive theory seems to give us the resources to meet the objection. In the 'bent stick' case, we do come to acquire an actual, currently present, cognitive structure very like an ordinary perception. Its intentional structure, moreover, is the same as a through-and-through veridical perception of something bent. Compare telling a story that both narrator and audience know perfectly well is false. The story-teller's words and thoughts and the audience's thoughts do not lose their intentionality just because everybody knows that the teller is not telling the truth. We do not attribute truth to the story-teller's tale; and we do not attribute veridicality to the perception of the stick as bent.

The mind is a big place, and it contains many programs and many modules. One great program, with innumerable sub-programs, is the perceptual program. It is a completely invaluable program for steering in the world. Without it we could not live. But we get to know that, as a guide to the state of our body and the world, it has certain limitations. It is like a set of trusted and efficient spies who continuously send back reports on what is going on. But it becomes known at headquarters that in certain limited situations reports come back that are flawed in certain ways. Headquarters, which is responsible for initiating action in the light of present circumstances, discounts these reports, overruling the *prima facie* attributions made by the spies.

We come now to the most serious of all the objections to a cognitivist theory of perception, the one on which I think John Foster would also put the most weight. It may be called 'the Argument from the Secondary Qualities', where these qualities are the qualities of color, of sound, of taste, of smell, of heat and cold and perhaps certain other qualities associated with bodily perception. Foster argues, with a good deal of plausibility, that our ordinary conceptions of these qualities involve a contradiction that is not easy to resolve.

The first point is that, as a matter of phenomenology, these qualities belong in the physical world. They characterize physical objects or physical phenomena. I suppose that the clearest case is surface color. The colors, including white and black, when they characterize surfaces seem very clearly to be intrinsic (non-relational) properties of these surfaces. As it has been said, they are 'painted on' the surfaces. The details of the phenomenology of the other secondary qualities are perhaps less clear, but we do seem to place them in the world. The sound fills the room or comes from one corner, the smell hangs around, the taste is there in the object as it meets the tongue, the hotness or coldness of the water is there in the water.

(Interestingly, the point is to be found in Berkeley, although in the service of his Idealism. In the *First Dialogue* he asks, "if you will trust your senses, is it not plain that all sensible qualities co-exist, or to them appear as being in the same place? Do they ever represent a motion, of figure, as being divested of all other visible and tangible qualities?")

Yet at the same time, how can the secondary qualities qualify the physical world? There are two arguments to be noted here. One is particularly familiar, and may be called 'the Argument from Science' or the 'Argument from Physics'. I think that I only need to gesture at it here. We seem to have good reasons for excluding these qualities from the physical world because they have no natural place in our developed conception of it. Foster does not put weight on this argument, rightly from his point of view because he is arguing for an Idealist or Berkeleyan conception of the physical world. But it has great weight with me.

Foster develops a more purely philosophical argument, which must also be given weight. He concedes that with respect to these qualities we can distinguish between a veridical and an illusory perception of them. There can be a question about what the color of a surface really is, and so on. But, he argues, this distinction, in contrast with the primary properties, is quite superficial. In the case of the secondary qualities, veridical perception is no more than what subjectively appears to a percipient in standard conditions.

We have, then, reasons to put the secondary qualities in the physical world, and reasons not to put them there. I would like to argue that we should go along with the idea that secondary qualities are where they are perceived to be. They are, however, not something over and above the primary properties—whatever science eventually decides the latter are. The secondary properties are really microphysical properties. They are not additional to the primary properties, but are certain microphysical properties imperfectly, or as Leibniz would say, confusedly perceived. If this can be made plausible, then it will be seen that the argument from physics becomes no objection. I think it will emerge that Foster's argument can also be answered.

It is surprising that this *realistic reductionism* about the secondary qualities has its best classical upholder in Leibniz, for whom the physical world is no better than a 'well-founded phenomenon'. The best quotation I have found is from his *New Essays on Human Understanding* (Leibniz, 1981). Locke had argued that there is no resemblance between pain and the motion of a piece of steel dividing our flesh. But Leibniz says:

> It is true that pain does not resemble the movement of a pin; but it might thoroughly resemble the motions which the pin causes in our body, and might represent them in the soul; and I have not the least doubt that it does. That is why we say the pain is in our body and not in the pin, although we say that the light is in the fire; because there are motions in the fire which the senses cannot clearly detect individually, but which form a confusion—a running together—which is brought within the reach of the senses and is represented to us by the idea of light. (Leibniz, 132)

Again, he says:

> The ideas ... of sensible qualities retain their place among the simple ideas only because of our ignorance. [The sensible qualities only appear simple.] (Leibniz, 132)

Arguing in the spirit of Leibniz, I think of our perception of the secondary qualities as awarenesses of complex microphysical properties that we are unable to analyze in any way, so the properties present themselves to us as simple. We are aware of all sorts of intrinsic resemblances and differences among these properties, but not of the basis of these resemblances and differences. These properties are *biologically* very important properties for us and other animals to pick up, giving invaluable assistance in what Berkeley called 'the conduct of life'. But, ontologically speaking, these properties are complex, idiosyncratic, apparently very disjunctive in many cases, and quite fail to carve the noble beast that is the world along its property joints.

Since, furthermore, the properties are picked up in what may be called a *gestalt* fashion—the senses, for good and obvious reasons, being unable to penetrate to the real complexities involved—it is easy to see that the only way to experience these properties *in just the way we experience them* will be to have the use of our particular set of sense-organs. If so, then there is a sense in which the experienced properties have an existence relative to perceivers, although strictly it is only our experience of these properties that has this relative existence.

So, although there is no doubt that the secondary qualities constitute the chief problem that a cognitive theory of perception must confront, I think that this problem shows promise of having been solved.φ

Bibliography

Anscombe, G.E.M., "The Intentionality of Sensation: A Grammatical Feature," in ed. R.J. Butler, *Analytical Philosophy,* 2nd series (Oxford: Basil Blackwell, 1965).

Armstrong, D.M., *Perception and the Physical World* (London: Routledge & Kegan Paul, 1961).

Armstrong, D.M., *Bodily Sensations* (London: Routledge & Kegan Paul, 1962).

Armstrong, D.M., *A Materialist Theory of the Mind* (London: Routledge & Kegan Paul, 1968).

Foster, John, *The Nature of Perception* (Oxford: Oxford University Press, 2000).

Leibniz, G.W., *New Essays on Human Understanding,* ed. and trans. Peter Remnant and Jonathan Bennett (Cambridge: Cambridge University Press, 1981).

Martin, C.B. and Pfiefer, K., "Intentionality and the Non-Psychological," *Philosophy and Phenomenological Research,* vol. 46 (1986): 531-54.

Molnar, George, *Powers,* ed. Stephen Mumford (Oxford: Oxford University Press, 2003).

Reply To Armstrong

By John Foster

THE COGNITIVE THEORY OF PERCEPTION, OF WHICH DAVID ARMSTRONG IS the originator and most illustrious advocate, claims that sense perception consists in the acquisition of propositional information about the environment. In my book, *The Nature of Perception*, I argue that the theory is vulnerable to two main objections.

The first objection is that the theory cannot provide an adequate account of the psychological form in which the information is received. As Armstrong acknowledges, the reception need not involve the acquisition of an environmental belief, or set of beliefs, or even an inclination to such beliefs, since a subject may be convinced that his perceptual experience is non-veridical. On the other hand, it must involve more than just the entertaining of a certain proposition or set of propositions. As far as I can see, the only viable proposal is to think of the reception of the information as consisting in the occurrence of something that *invites* the subject to acquire the relevant belief or beliefs. But I do not see what this something could be other than a sensory experience of the kind that the cognitivist rejects.

The second objection is that, by taking it to involve nothing more than the acquisition of information, the cognitive theory fails to do justice to the phenomenological character of perception. In particular, it does not explain why perception gives its subject the impression of being the (non-conceptual) presentation of something. It is not enough for the cognitivist to appeal here to the non-inferential character of perceptually acquired information, since the clairvoyant (non-perceptual) acquisition of information would also be non-inferential. As I see it, the only satisfactory way of explaining the presentational feel of perceptual experience is by supposing, contrary to the theory, that such experience actually is, in part, presentational. How this presentational approach should be developed is something that I discuss in detail in my book.

These, then, are what I see as the two main objections to the cognitive theory, and it seems to me that Armstrong's latest attempt to defend the theory does nothing to meet them. Indeed, it does not, as far as I can see, even address them.

One issue that Armstrong does address concerns the nature of the secondary qualities, and I shall end by briefly commenting on what he says. In my book, I try to show that these qualities, in their sensible form, are ones that achieve their realization in (and exclusively in) the content of sensory experience, and this conclusion too is in conflict with the cognitive theory. My argument for the conclusion is too complex to be summarized here. Armstrong thinks that he can meet it by taking the relevant qualities to be really microphysical properties, but ones that are, as he puts it, 'imperfectly', or 'confusedly', perceived. This puzzles me. If the microphysical properties are imperfectly or confusedly perceived, there must surely be certain other qualitative items that they are perceived as—other qualitative items that, in being perceived in that distorting way, they have the appearance of being. But I do not see what these qualitative items could be except the secondary qualities themselves—the very qualities, like sensible color and sensible temperature, that Armstrong wants to construe as microphysical. φ

A Green Thought in a Green Shade

By C.L. Hardin

YELLOW SUN IN A BLUE SKY. GREEN LEAVES CARESSED BY THE WIND. Open the shutters of the eye, that window of the soul, and all such things are revealed. Nothing is more apparent than that things have colors, and that we have immediate perceptual access to those colors.

But are the colors that we suppose objects to possess the same as the colors to which we have such ready access? Physics describes the color-relevant properties of objects in such quantitative terms as 'surface spectral reflectance' and '580 nanometers.' These predicates capture features of objects that are fit to play a causal role. The colors of which we are perceptually aware, on the other hand, receive qualitative descriptors such as 'red' and 'chartreuse.' They are conspicuously absent in causal accounts.

We seem to have two domains here. Can they be joined? Can we establish a regular set of connections between, say, a particular spectral reflectance—or another complex of physical properties—and a particular perceived color, perhaps a sufficiently intimate connection to warrant our asserting that the perceived color is identical with that spectral reflectance or physical complex? The stock philosophical mantra for dealing with the problem is that an object has color C just in case the object looks C to a normal (or standard) observer under normal (or standard) conditions. Not so long ago, this seemed to be an unproblematic principle, and some philosophers still regard it as unproblematic. The tacit assumption was that the lighting condition is to be daylight and the observer one who is not color deficient.

But which daylight? Morning, noon, or afternoon? Sunlight or north daylight? And what shall we say about the colors on television sets or computer monitors? Is daylight the best way to judge them? The vaunted constancy of colors under various lighting conditions is really only approximate, and many artificial colorants are in fact highly

C.L. Hardin is Professor Emeritus of Philosophy at Syracuse University. He is the author of Color for Philosophers: Unweaving the Rainbow *and coeditor, with ecological anthropologist Luisa Maffi, of* Color Categories in Thought and Language. *Currently he is ruminating on a Spinozistic account of the relation between mind and body.*

inconstant with simple changes in illuminant. When a material looks to have different colors under different reasonable, or "normal," illuminants, how are we to determine which of the different color appearances corresponds to the "true" color of the object?

Our present concern, however, is not with the "normal conditions" clause of our philosophical mantra, but with the "normal observer" clause. Given a certain amount of variability among actual normal observers, a sensible move would be to take a statistical average of them and construct an official, artificial "Standard Observer." This is just what the Commission Internationale de l'Eclairage (CIE) did in 1931. Refined and improved upon over the years, the specifications that constitute the Standard Observer and its corresponding standard illuminants and standard viewing conditions have been invaluable for industrial applications. But their limits are well understood. First of all, to quote the authoritative handbook of Wyszecki and Stiles,

> The problem of specifying object-color perceptions has not yet been solved for the general case in which the observer views a complicated scene composed of a large variety of objects. Various visual phenomena, such as simultaneous contrast, successive contrast, color constancy, memory color, size, and shape of the objects, come into play and contribute significantly to the resultant color perception of the complicated scene; but the science of color has not advanced far enough to deal with this problem quantitatively.[1]

Secondly, the Standard Observer is silent about color appearance. From it we can learn when two samples will or will not seem to match in color for the Standard Observer, and, if they fail to match, we can gain an estimate of how different they are. But it will not tell us how a sample's hue changes as it becomes brighter, or dimmer, or more or less saturated. In an important respect, then, the Standard Observer fails to capture the *quality* of color. If the eye is the window of the soul, the Standard Observer doesn't do windows.

Finally, simply because it is a statistical construct, the Standard Observer will fail to capture individual variations in color matching, variations that are surprisingly extensive. Fifty-five years ago, Ralph Evans remarked,

> A rough estimate indicates that a perfect match by a perfect "average" observer would probably be unsatisfactory for something like 90 percent of all observers because variation between observers is very much greater than the smallest color differences which they can distinguish. Any observer whose variation from the standard was much greater than his ability to distinguish differences would be dissatisfied with the match.[2]

It is now possible to determine the extent of matching differences among normal observers and to gain some insight into the causes of the variation.[3] Using an instrument called the anomaloscope, a standard instrument for diagnosing color deficiencies, color-normal observers are asked to match an orange test hemifield with a mixture hemifield of red and green primaries in which the observer can set the red/green ratio. For men, the distribution of ratios is bimodal, falling into two distinct groups, with 60% of the observers in one group and 40% in the other. The distribution of ratios for women is unimodal, and broader than that for men. In the last decade it has been shown that these distributions are correlated with genetically based polymorphisms of longwave and middlewave cone photopigments. Here we have a clear case of quantifiable, biologically based individual variations in color perceptions for normal observers under rigorously controlled standard conditions. No scientific sense can be attached to the claim that some of the observers are perceiving the color of the stimulus correctly and others not.

The match that an observer makes between the two hemifields of an anomaloscope is a metameric match. The two sides have different spectra, but when the match is made, they look identical. Although metameric matches are rare in nature, they are very common in the modern world; the images of color photography and color television are metameric or approximately metameric matches to the color appearances of the objects that they represent. Because of inevitable variations in viewing conditions and in observers, such matches are to one degree or another problematic and rely on the large reservoir of forgiveness that the human brain has for color variation when the samples are not put side by side.

This issue is important in evaluating those philosophical theories of color that put colors outside the head. For example, Alex Byrne and David Hilbert[4] hold that surface colors are to be identified with classes of spectral reflectances that yield the same color appearance. Since they want to distinguish between the real and the apparent colors of objects, they need to establish a criterion for membership in a set of reflectances that are to count as the same real color. Because color appearances are a function of both viewing conditions and observers, they must establish normative conditions for both of these. I think that we are entitled to require that the choice of these conditions depend upon a set of reasonable principles. In the case of normal observers, whose color matches are to count as the correct matches; that is, which colors actually match and which colors only appear to match? I own a metameric slide rule, a device that has two sliding colored scales that may be independently adjusted. The observer moves the scales so that the portions of the two scales that can be seen through the window match to a close approximation. Change the illuminant, and the scales must be readjusted to yield a match. Keep the illuminant the same but change the observer, and quite often the match that satisfies the one normal observer will be seen by another normal observer as a gross mismatch. It will not surprise you to learn that when I adjusted the scales for a match that satisfied me, it failed to satisfy David Hilbert, and when he found a satisfactory match, I saw the colors of the scales as markedly different. My match was, of course, the correct one; Hilbert was the victim of a color illusion!

Actually, given my principles, I am as comfortable with Hilbert's match as I am with my own, but, given his principles, at least one of us must be wrong. But in that case, how would he proceed to decide the issue?

Color matching has to do with a judgment as to whether two color stimuli are seen as the same or as different. It does not tell us anything about the qualities of the colors that we experience; nor does it tell us into what categories they fall. It does not tell us whether the stimuli are red or blue, orange or brown; nor does it tell us why purples are more like red than like green. It is only by using our eyes that we can learn these things. If we wish to assign colors to stimuli, we must do so empirically, by discovering which sorts of stimuli bring about which sorts of color experiences. Given a particular observer in a particular state of adaptation and a particular set of observational conditions, there is a way to do this. The names of just four perceptually basic hues—red, yellow, green, and blue—are both necessary and sufficient to describe every hue.[5] The description of a hue is given in terms of its degree of resemblance to one pair of these basic hues. The four basic hues are called *unique* hues. A unique hue contains no perceptual traces of other hues. Thus, a unique green is a green that is neither yellowish nor bluish, a unique blue is a hue that is neither reddish nor greenish, and so on. By contrast, no purple can be a unique hue, since every purple is both reddish and bluish.

Vision scientists use two ways of determining what colors people see. One of them is to ask them to judge the degree of resemblance to unique hues. This is commonly called 'hue naming'. The other, the 'cancellation technique', requires them to adjust the amount of a light of fixed wavelength so as to cancel the component of a target light that is complementary to the light of fixed wavelength. Thus a fixed light seen by the subject to be a unique blue may be used to cancel the yellowish component of a target light, for example one that appears orange. When the cancellation is complete, the light that originally looked orange will appear to the observer to be a desaturated red. Iterated across the spectrum, the cancellation technique will generate the opponent response function for the observer in question. Jack Werner and Billy Wooten showed that the average hue naming by observers is closely correlated with their opponent response as given by the cancellation technique.[6] Furthermore, the cancellation technique gives results that can also be calculated from color-matching data. So the color names that people give to stimuli are strongly, though indirectly, correlated to their execution of a behavioral task.

Since our old friend, the CIE Standard Observer, is a set of color-matching functions, we might now suppose that he might be pressed into service as a color categorizer. If so, we could use him objectively to classify all manner of surface spectral reflectances in terms of red, yellow, green, and blue. He would enable us to specify the unique hues and distinguish them from the binary hues. We could objectively determine classes of metamers.

Well, almost. But is almost good enough here? After all, the CIE Standard Observer is also known as the CIE Average Observer and, as such, is going to perform like some, but by no means all, real observers. As we have seen, real observers differ from each other in their color-matching and metameric classes, so it should come as no surprise that their opponent responses are different. Even small differences are of considerable significance for realist theories of color, for realists must shoulder the burden of deciding in a non-arbitrary fashion which normal observers are seeing colors as they really are and which ones are misperceiving them.

In fact, the differences are large enough to be shocking, as we shall now see. The stimulus locus for a perception of unique hue has been studied with a variety of techniques for many years. Every study with a reasonably large number of observers has found a wide distribution of unique hue loci among normal perceivers. Because the studies have used different experimental protocols, the mean results do not agree well across experiments, but substantial variability among observers within any given study is a constant. It is generally accepted that more "naturalistic" experiments using surface colors will reduce the amount of variance from one observer to another, so I shall present you with the results of some unique hue experiments with colored Munsell papers that were recently done by Rolf Kuehni.[7] He used a 40-step hue set. The Munsell chips are approximately perceptually equispaced, so each chip

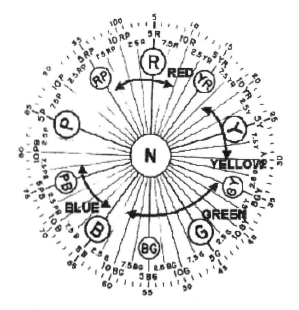

is 1/40 of the hue circle. The figure shows the range of unique hue choices from experiments with two subject pools.

The male and female distributions are generally markedly different, and neither one approximates a Gaussian distribution for any of the hues. Even if the gender results are taken separately, no single chip will represent the unique hue choice of a majority of observers for a given hue category. The range of variability persists even when the choices of the least consistent observers are discarded. Furthermore, the unique hue choices of each individual are very stable over time.

There are approximately 10 distinct hue perceptions between two Munsell 40-Hue steps, so the unique red hue range of six steps works out to roughly 60 distinguishable hue differences. If the results for the four unique hue ranges are taken together, there fails to be consensus on 26 out of a total of the 40 chips composing the hue circle. Sixty percent of the hue circle is in dispute! We could arrive at a more conservative estimate by taking the results of a single set of experiments on the grounds that differences in the experimental protocols are likely to make for greater variability in outcomes. But even if we do this, there is no consensus on 16 of the 40 chips, a forty percent disagreement.

When the facts about the variability of color perception among normal observers are pointed out to defenders of color realism, one common response is that there may be disagreements about particular, determinate colors, but there is certainly agreement about determinable colors. We can all agree, for instance, that a particular object is red. Well, yes and no. It is true that all of the normal observers will call most of the chips in the unique red range 'red', most of the chips in the unique green range 'green', and so on. But just how far does consensus go in color naming? Sturges and Whitfield[8] examined color naming of a large sample of the Munsell color solid with responses from twenty subjects. Less than 1/4 of the chips were named with both consistency and consensus. If we consider just the hue dimension, we notice that the ranges for the judgments of unique hues and the consensus judgments for the four basic colors correspond pretty closely. But the consensus colors form islands in a sea of non-consensus color naming. In particular, there is a pronounced gap in the hue range between the consensus green chips and the consensus blue chips that confirms the everyday observation that people commonly disagree about whether a particular color in this range is "really" green or "really" blue. So what is the determinable that covers this range? Grue? Actually, many languages lack separate basic color terms for green and blue, using an omnibus term to cover the whole blue-or-green range. There is, however, no known language with a basic term, that is, a term used with high consistency and consensus, that covers this intermediate region as 'orange' covers the hue region between red and yellow.

Should the realist content himself with the observation that all of us can agree that an object falling in this region is blue-or-green? The obvious rejoinder is that such an object falls under the determinables "bluish" and "greenish." This is perfectly true, but now we must ask whether we can generally agree of a given object whether or not it falls under a determinable such as "bluish." Take, for example, the Munsell chip 7.5G seen under the artificial daylight of Kuehni's second unique green experiment. Twenty-three observers judged it to be bluish, but fourteen observers judged it to be neither bluish nor yellowish, and six observers saw it as yellowish. It seems that we cannot secure agreement on the extension of this determinable, though each particular person can determine that extension with a high degree of reliability. The argument can be repeated for each of the determinables red, yellow, and blue as well. But the extensions of these cover the entire hue space.

In the face of the facts of individual differences in color perception, realists such as Alex Byrne, David Hilbert, and Michael Tye take the position that some normal perceivers see colors as they are, whereas others perceive them erroneously. If the differences in perception were indeed small, we might be willing to keep them in the closet. But, as we have seen, the differences are simply too large for such a "don't ask, don't tell" policy. Not only must some substantial numbers of normal perceivers be significantly misperceiving, they must be chronically misperceiving. For his part, Michael Tye[9] is unfazed by this result. Perceptual errors of shape and temperature are common, says he, but we do not therefore suppose that shapes and temperatures are not features of the physical world. Our epistemic difficulties in determining the true colors of surfaces do not threaten the objective status of these colors.

So here's the part where that which has been given by one hand is taken away by the other. Much of the initial appeal of color realism was that colors seem to be presented directly to perception in all of their naked glory. Now, it appears that multitudes of us must content ourselves with knowing about colors indirectly. For us unfortunate souls, the veil of perception has been restored. Those of us who sometimes misperceive shapes and temperatures have recourse to instruments such as thermometers and rulers to correct ourselves, but we who misperceive unique green have no alternative ways of rectifying our false judgements. Byrne and Hilbert are prepared to accept this result, and cheerfully tell us that they are prepared to countenance "unknowable color facts."

Shades of Lord Kelvin! You will recall his pronouncement at the end of the nineteenth century that physics is essentially complete, there being but "two small clouds on the horizon," namely, the black-body problem and the negative result of the Michelson-Morley experiment. From these clouds quantum mechanics and relativity theory were to emerge. Defenders of the old order took refuge in unknowable facts about absolute velocity and determinate trajectories. Others, however, took the epistemological challenge to heart. They saw that a theory requiring unknowable facts is a theory that rests on questionable assumptions.

There is another brand of realism, notably advocated by Brian McLaughlin and Jonathan Cohen,[10] that has learned these lessons of

modern physics. Its rallying cry is "Relativize!" Does the color that you
see depend upon the illumination? Relativize! Does the color that you
see depend upon the surroundings? Relativize! Does the color that you
see depend upon your state of adaptation and the fact that it is your eyes
that see it? Once again, relativize! A surface has a color K, not simpliciter,
but rather with respect to conditions C and illuminant L for observer O
under the state of adaptation A. Thus, every surface has as many colors
as these parameters have values. Indeed, for every counterexample X,
we need only add parameter X'.

Will this device work? It is difficult to see how it could fail to do
so. Indeed, it will work all too well. To me, this woman's face is the very
form of beauty incarnate. To Jonathan, it is a face that only a blind mother
could love. Beauty is in the eye of the beholder, you say? No, it is an
objective property of the woman's face, for I only need to relativize it to
Larry's gaze, if only at time T. Ugliness is also an objective property of
her face, provided of course we understand it as being relative to
Jonathan's eye at time T. And so this same woman has the possibility of
being all things to all men.

Beyond that, the plurality of color properties that the relativist
generates is just too reminiscent (if I may use this word) of Gorgias'
definition of virtue as related by Meno:

> First of all, if it is manly virtue you are after, it is easy to see that the virtue of
> a man consists in managing the city's affairs capably, and so that he will help
> his friends and injure his foes while taking care to come to no harm himself.
> Or if you want a woman's virtue, that is easily described. She must be a good
> housewife, careful with her stores and obedient to her husband. Then there is
> another virtue for a child, male or female, and another for an old man, free or
> slave as you like; and a great many more kinds of virtue, so that no one need
> be at a loss to say what it is. For every act and every time of life, with
> reference to each separate function, there is a virtue for each one of us, and
> similarly, I should say, a vice.[11]

To which Socrates exclaims: "How fortunate I am, Meno! I wanted one
virtue and I find that you have a whole swarm of virtues to offer." Here
we have it: Must we choose between Byrne's cryptic colors and Cohen's
chromatic swarm?

I think that we can avoid both. Let us look at what we can agree
upon. We agree that the colors that we see are typically caused by the
spectral power distributions that affect our eyes. There are no mysteries
here, and no ungainly pluralities either. We agree on the basic
mechanisms within our brains that process, categorize, and transform
these stimuli. The net result of the workings of these mechanisms is in
plain view, although the detailed nature of the mechanisms is something
of which we are largely, though not entirely, ignorant. It is those
mechanisms rather than the stimuli on which they operate that give
unity and simplicity to the colors of experience. We also agree that the
objects of chromatic seeing are not colored mental items, variously called

'sensations' or 'sense-data'.

Where we might not agree is that color experience is qualitative, and that the same qualitative character can be present in experience even in the absence of the usual external stimuli. As I understand them, some color realists such as Gilbert Harman have maintained that we are directly aware of object color and that all color experience is to be explicated in terms of propositions about the colors of objects along with the notion of intentionality. If successful, such a maneuver would rid us of the qualia problem. Because I find a physical object's having a color to be a problematic notion, I do not think that the problem of qualitative content can be avoided.

Very well. But if physical objects aren't colored, and there are no mental color bearers, just where does color reside? My response is that color properties don't reside anywhere, because we don't need to suppose that there are any. What we do need to suppose is that we experience surfaces and lights and volumes as colored, which means that we must have experiences of a qualitative character. Most realists not of Harman's persuasion will grant that our experiences do have qualitative character. Just how that character is realized by our neural wetware is of course a very difficult question. I do not think that it is by any means an unsolvable question, or a question that goes beyond the resources of the science of the future, but it is in any event a question with which realists must also deal. My point is simply that since our world has both spectral power distributions and primate nervous systems, it doesn't also need colors.

The seventeenth-century poet Andrew Marvell,[12] having decided that he had neither world enough nor time, gave up pursuing his coy mistress and found solace in gardening:

> When we have run our passion's heat,
> Love hither makes his best retreat.
> The gods, that mortal beauty chase,
> Still in a tree did end their race:
> Apollo hunted Daphne so,
> Only that she might laurel grow;
> And Pan did after Syrinx speed,
> Not as a nymph, but for a reed.

And then came his insight into the nature of color:

> Meanwhile the mind, from pleasure less,
> Withdraws into its happiness;
> The mind, that ocean where each kind
> Does straight its own resemblance find,
> Yet it creates, transcending these,
> Far other worlds, and other seas;
> Annihilating all that's made
> To a green thought in a green shade.

I owe it to my colleagues in the Department of Textual Studies to deconstruct these last two lines. What is to be annihilated is of course the world of color properties, fabricated or "made" by color realists, with green serving as surrogate for all of the colors. "Thought" must be understood in the omnibus Cartesian sense, as covering all mental happenings; in this instance, "thought" means "visual perception." To call a thought, which we have now glossed as "perception," green, is permissible poetic license; the literal meaning of the phrase is "a perception as of green" or, better yet, "a perceiving greenly." "In" can only be understood in the constitutive sense, and the "a" in "a green shade" should be understood as a free variable, ranging over the shades of green.

This exegesis does not measure up to the elevated scholarly standards of Textual Studies, but I believe that Marvell, as a metaphysical poet, would have wanted a philosopher to make his thoughts more accessible to an audience of the twenty-first century. So here are the last lines of "The Garden," as amended:

> Annihilating all the false colors that realists have made
> To a perceiving greenly, as a constituent of each green shade.

You didn't expect philosophy to scan, did you? φ

Notes

[1] Wyszecki, G. and W.S. Stiles, *Color Science: Concepts and Methods, Quantitative Data and Formulae*, 2nd ed. (New York: John Wiley and Sons, 1982), 173.

[2] Evans, R.M., *An Introduction to Color* (New York: John Wiley and Sons, 1948), 196-7.

[3] Neitz, M. and J. Neitz, "Molecular Genetics and the Biological Basis of Color Vision," in eds. W. G. K. Backhaus, R. Kliegl, and J. S. Werner, *Colour Vision: Perspectives from Different Disciplines* (Berlin: Walter de Gruyter, 1998), 101-119.

[4] Byrne, A. and D. Hilbert, "Color Realism and Color Science," *Behavioral and Brain Sciences*, vol. 26, no. 1 (2003): 3-21.

[5] Sternheim, C.S. and R. M. Boynton, "Uniqueness of Perceived Hues Investigated with a Continuous Judgmental Technique," *Journal of Experimental Psychology*, vol. 72, no. 5 (1966): 770-776.

[6] Werner, J.S. and B.S. Wooten, "Opponent Chromatic Mechanisms: Relation to Photopigments and Hue Naming," *Journal of the Optical Society of America*, vol. 69 (1979): 422-434.

[7] Kuehni, R.G, "Determination of Unique Hues Using Munsell Color Chips," *Color Research and Application*, vol. 26 (2001): 61-66. Also see "Variability in Perception of Color Stimuli by Color-normal Humans" on Kuehni's web page, www.4nscu.edu/~rgkuehni. Also see Webster, M.A., "Variations in Normal Color Vision. II. Unique Huques," *Journal of the Optical Society of America A*, vol. 9 (2000): 1545-1555.

[8] Sturgis, J. and T. W. A. Whitfield, "Locating Basic Colours in the Munsell Space," *Color Research and Application*, vol. 20, no. 6 (1995): 364-376.

[9] Tye, M., *Consciousness, Color, and Content* (Cambridge: MIT Press, 2000).

[10] McLaughlin, B., "The Place of Color in Nature," in eds. R. Mausfeld and D. Heyer, *Colour: Connecting the Mind to the Physical World* (Oxford: Oxford University Press,

2003), 475-505. Also see Cohen, J., "Color: A Functionalist Proposal," *Philosophical Studies*, vol. 113, no. 1 (2003): 1-42.

[11] Plato, *Meno*, 71E., trans. W. K. C. Guthrie, in eds. Edith Hamilton and Huntingdon Cairns, *The Collected Dialogues of Plato*, Bollingen Series LXXI (Princeton: Princeton University Press, 1961).

[12] Marvell, Andrew (1621-1678). The poems from which the quotations are taken are "To His Coy Mistress" and "The Garden."

Structuralism and the Independence of Mathematics

By Michael D. Resnik

> Considered relative to our surface irritations, which exhaust our clues to an external world, the molecules and their extraordinary ilk are thus much on a par with the most ordinary physical objects. The positing of these extraordinary things is just a vivid analogue of the positing or acknowledging of ordinary things: vivid in that the physicist audibly posits them for recognized reasons, whereas the hypothesis of ordinary things is shrouded in prehistory....
>
> To call a posit a posit is not to patronize it.... Everything to which we concede existence is a posit from the standpoint of a description of the theory-building process, and simultaneously real from the standpoint of the theory that is being built. (W. V. Quine)[1]

Mathematical objects, if they exist at all, exist independently of our proofs, constructions, and stipulations. For example, whether inaccessible cardinals exist or not, the very act of our proving or postulating that they do doesn't make it so. This independence thesis is a central claim of mathematical realism. It is also one that many anti-realists acknowledge too. For they agree that we cannot create mathematical truths or objects, though, to be sure, they deny that mathematical objects exist at all. I have defended a mathematical realism of sorts. I interpret the objects of mathematics as positions in patterns (or structures, if you will), and maintain that they exist independently of us, and our stipulations, proofs, and the like.

By taking mathematical objects to be positions in patterns I see all mathematical objects as being like geometrical points in having no identifying features save those arising through the relations they bear to other mathematical objects in the structures to which they belong. Mathematicians talk of numbers, functions, sets, and spaces in order to depict structures. Thus they might describe the natural number sequence (0, 1, 2, etc.) as the smallest number structure that has exactly one number (position) immediately following each of its numbers (positions) as well

Michael D. Resnik is University Distinguished Professor of Philosophy at the University of North Carolina at Chapel Hill. He has written about logic, the philosophy of mathematics, and the theory of rational decision making. His most important writings include Frege and the Philosophy of Mathematics, Mathematics as a Science of Patterns, *and* Choices: An Introduction to Decision Theory.

as an initial number (position), call it '0', which is preceded by no other numbers (positions) in the structure. One of the important features of patterns is that they may occur or be embedded in other patterns. Take for example, simple songs. The pattern of notes exhibited in their initial verses usually recurs in subsequent verses. Furthermore, if we transpose the song into different keys, then the pattern of musical intervals occurs again and again in each new key, with each transposition being a different pattern of notes. I see mathematicians as making observations similar to these, as well as abstracting patterns from practical experience, finding occurrences of patterns in each other, and "combining" patterns to arrive at new ones.

Structuralist views of mathematical objects, of which mine is just one, have a reputable history among mathematicians that dates to at least the 1870s.[2] Dedekind expounded a version of structuralism, and we can find kindred themes in Hilbert too. But the recent spate of structuralist writings in the philosophy of mathematics has been in response to two influential papers by Paul Benacerraf, "What numbers could not be" (1965) and "Mathematical truth" (1973).[3] In the first paper Benacerraf reflected on the variety of ways mathematicians have found for defining the natural numbers as sets.[4] Noting that these definitions are equally good from a mathematical point of view, he concluded that there is no fact as to which sets the numbers are, and consequently, that numbers are not sets at all. This was contrary to the teachings of Frege and Russell and many subsequent analytic philosophers, but Benacerraf continued with a more radical thought. Claiming that number theory is just the theory of a certain structure and that numbers have no identifying features except structural ones, he inferred that numbers are not objects at all, or as he put it, "if the truth be known, there are no such things as numbers; which is not to say that there are not at least two prime numbers between 15 and 20."[5]

I found myself unwilling to follow Benacerraf in his last step. His argument that number theory is the science of a certain structure was convincing, but unless something exhibits that structure, number theory is vacuous. Moreover, Benacerraf's observations applied to all of mathematics. For throughout mathematics we find alternative (and incompatible) definitions of important mathematical objects. Real numbers may be defined as sets or as infinite sequences or as the sums of infinite series, functions may be defined in terms of sets or sets in terms of functions, and so on. Mathematics may well be the science of structure, but lest it be vacuous, the ontological buck most stop somewhere—things exhibiting the various mathematical structures must exist.[6]

Benacerraf's "Mathematical truth" emphasized a different but much older problem. In the history of the philosophy of mathematics we find views that present a plausible account of mathematical truth by positing a mathematical ontology of abstract entities and views that present a plausible account of mathematical knowledge by emphasizing the role that symbol manipulation and proof play in mathematical practice. Yet nowhere can we find a plausible account of both mathematical truth and mathematical knowledge. If mathematics is about abstract entities that exist outside of space and time, then it's an utter mystery as to how we can access them and acquire mathematical knowledge. (This is the 'Access Problem'.) On the other hand, if we solve the Access Problem by taking the subject matter of mathematics to be symbols and proofs, we cannot account for the truth of mathematical sentences that purport to make claims about numbers, functions, sets and the like; for we know, thanks to logicians like Frege and Quine, that it is just a confusion to think that these are just symbols. So we are left with a dilemma: we can have a reasonable account of mathematical truth or a reasonable account of mathematical knowledge but not both.

But if we think of mathematical objects as like positions in patterns, then we may be able to solve both of Benacerraf's problems. For just as geometrical points have no identifying features — they all "look alike" — except the ones they have by virtue of their relationships to other geometrical objects, positions in patterns have no identifying features save those which they have in virtue of their relationships to other positions. This would explain why mathematicians don't care whether they define the numbers one way or another so long as the structure of the numbers is preserved, and it would explain why there is no fact of the matter as to whether the numbers are sets. That's just the way positions are. There is a lot more to my interpretation of mathematical objects as positions in patterns than I have presented here, but I want to leave it to discuss my approach to Benacerraf's other problem.[7]

Now one might think that we can access positions through accessing the structures or patterns containing them, and one might also think that something like pattern recognition would be a reliable means for so doing. Some of my earlier papers suggest such an approach, and I know through correspondence and conversation that the idea has found a number of friends. But recently I have not held such a view, and I am not sure that I ever have. Put loosely, I admit patterns that are not concretely instantiated. Now, perhaps, we come to know things about patterns by initially learning things about concretely instantiated ones. But even if this is true, I don't think it will be of much help in accounting for our knowledge of mathematical objects themselves. For mathematical objects, that is, the positions in patterns themselves are very abstract objects, and it is unclear how they could be presented to us by means of the more concrete things occupying them. At least it is unclear how they could be presented to us via an undoubtedly natural process. This is just a structuralist version of the Access Problem.

I don't see how you can avoid foundering on this problem if you face it directly. We have no causal access to mathematical objects or anything that could be taken to be their traces, since they have no traces. For the same reason we don't even have such access to structures though their instances or to types through their tokens. Of course, we often take instances of patterns and tokens of types to reflect features of the patterns and types themselves. For example, speaking of a letter qua type, we might say, "the letter 'A' looks like this," and then inscribe a token 'A'. But letter types are abstract entities, and as such they don't reflect light; so we "see" them only in an extended sense, and can never directly test hypotheses concerning their relation to their tokens.

In my book, *Mathematics as Science of Patterns*, I approached the Access Problem by applying a postulational epistemology to mathematics. My account had two parts. The first addressed the question of how the first mathematicians could have acquired mathematical beliefs without encountering mathematical objects. This question had puzzled many people influenced by the Access Problem. In answering it I hypothesized that developing, manipulating and studying notations for representing systems of concrete objects eventually led ancient mathematicians to posit mathematical objects qua abstract positions in structures. The second part of my account explained how these beliefs, though initially acquired in a way that need not generate knowledge, could indeed count as knowledge, and why standard contemporary mathematics is a body of knowledge too.

The second part of my epistemology is a pragmatic version of confirmational holism—the idea, originating in Duhem and extended by Quine, that hypotheses are confirmed or refuted in bundles rather than individually. The version I favor distinguishes between global (or holistic) conceptions of evidence and pragmatically grounded local conceptions of evidence. The basic idea is that from a logical point of view data will typically bear directly only globally upon relatively large systems of hypotheses, yet we can be pragmatically justified in taking certain data to bear upon a specific hypothesis. Biologists, for example, will be pragmatically justified in appealing to a conception of evidence local to biology to conclude, say, that a certain study refutes a certain biological hypothesis. They need not concern themselves with the fact that from the logical point of view the study also bears upon broader biological, chemical and physical hypotheses and the statistical methods they used. In applying these ideas to mathematics, I take its numerous applications to provide global evidence for mathematics, but I countenance local evidence for mathematical theories too. Indeed, as I see it, a hierarchy of (local) evidence for mathematics parallels the evidential hierarchy of the other sciences. Just as bits of elementary chemistry can support sub-atomic physics, some of the results of arithmetic and geometry can be tested against computations and measurements, analysis can be supported via its arithmetic and geometric consequences, more abstract theories confirmed via their consequences for analysis, and so on. Furthermore, I doubt that the local conception of evidence frees mathematicians from worries about whether the objects they posit exist. The history of the controversies over the negative, imaginary, and infinite numbers, infinitesimals, impredicative sets, and choice functions show that they frequently do concern themselves with the status of newly introduced mathematical entities, and try to find considerations favoring their existence.

I coupled this epistemology with notions of truth and reference that are immanent and disquotational. This means that they apply only to our own language, and serve primarily to permit inferences such as the following:

1) Everything Tess said is true, and she said, "Jones was at home", so Jones was at home.

2) The term "the Big Apple" is used to refer to New York City; thus, if the Big Apple is hectic, so is New York City.

Even this modest conception of truth and reference allows one to formulate theses committing one to an independent mathematical reality. (One such thesis is that classical mathematical analysis is true whether or not we have proven it to be so.) Moreover, it avoids worries about how our mathematical terms "hook onto" mathematical objects, and explains how initiating mathematical talk can enable us to refer to and describe objects to which we have no causal connection.

Further details of my account need not concern us now. But it is important for me to emphasize that two parts of my account are not tightly connected. It is true that after we have posited positions arranged in various patterns we can refer to them in order to interpret and make better sense of the experiences that led us to posit them. Moreover, I see these experiences as data that give some confirmation to the hypotheses postulating the positions. However, on my view, nothing in the course of positing, including having the experiences that motivated the positing, establishes the existence of the entities posited or the truth of the postulates concerning them. Exactly this feature of my epistemology has been the source of an important objection to it.

The problem is that in an important sense I turned my back on the Access Problem instead of solving it. I did show how we might have arrived at our mathematical beliefs through reasonable means and how they are part of a systematic whole that experience supports. But while this may show that our system of mathematical and scientific theories is internally coherent and squares with experience, it still does not show how mathematics connects to an independent reality.

Here is how Jody Azzouni has expressed his reservation:

Some philosophers of mathematics marry an ontologically independent mathematical realm to a stipulationist epistemology. The result is unstable if only because such a union still craves explanation for why the stipulations in question correspond to properties of the ontologically independent items they are stipulations about.[8]

Azzouni is confident that I cannot meet his demand for an explanation of how mathematics is tied to an independent reality, because the practice of science and mathematics "offers no epistemic role for mathematical objects, and so does not respond to the worry that there are no mathematical objects for its theorems to be true of."[9]

Here Azzouni has in mind his 'Epistemic Role Puzzle', that is, the puzzling fact that whether or not mathematical objects exist, they seem to play no role in the things mathematicians do to obtain mathematical knowledge. This is a cousin of the Access Problem; for if mathematical objects are abstract entities, then it's unclear how they could play any role in mathematical practice. Unlike the objects that usually concern science, we cannot interact with them or physically manipulate them.

Now there are two ways one might try to respond to the Epistemic Role Puzzle. First, one might explain why mathematical objects, by their very nature, could not and should not have an epistemic role; and then go on to argue that this still does not prevent us from having knowledge that is about them. This is what I tried to do in my book by interpreting mathematical objects as positions in patterns. Since it is the essence of a position that it has no function except to mark a place relative to other places in the pattern containing it, there is no basis for supposing that it has any properties that would allow us to detect it or manipulate it or otherwise involve it in our usual epistemic processes. Mathematics describes structures by telling how objects in them, that is, positions, are related. This is the only reason that it needs objects, and it requires no more of them than that they be related to each other in various ways. Thus in so far as mathematics concerns itself with structure and only structure, it is virtually pointless for its objects to have physically detectable features. Furthermore, if mathematics acknowledged any physical objects as its own proper objects, then it would be obliged to study their physical properties and would sacrifice its focus on structure. Thus, given the goals of mathematics, it makes sense for it to ignore questions of the physical nature of its objects. And given that it does, it is impossible for them to have any epistemic role in Azzouni's sense.

The second response would be to argue that in an indirect sense mathematical objects do indeed have an epistemic role. This is the sort of response that formalists who hold that mathematics is about formulas could make. Moreover, in a kind of convoluted way it is open to me too. For, on my view, some mathematical notations mirror the structures they represent. For example, a finite sequence of inscribed unary numerals instantiates an initial segment of an omega sequence; a paper and pencil Turing Machine computation instantiates its abstract counterpart as does a formal derivation or a triangle on a blackboard. So one might argue that here at least structures and their positions do have a role in obtaining mathematical knowledge. I can think of two objections to this response: a) the response appeals to the relationship between types and their tokens, and the former are clearly concrete, so it is they, and not the types which have an epistemic role; b) the response goes through only if we posit structural similarities between the types and tokens in question, and we have no independent way of confirming that these similarities exist.

Later I shall argue that we don't directly access physical objects either but rather only through connections that we posit linking them to sense experience. If this is correct, then neither objection (*a*) nor objection (*b*) is compelling.

Let us assume for now that that I can respond successfully to the Epistemic Role Puzzle. I still don't think this sets to rest the general worry about my view. Ultimately, we may have a conflict between what Azzouni calls "coherentist epistemic positions"[10] and more foundational approaches. On the coherentist approach, if our current overall theory of the world is empirically adequate and meets other epistemic virtues, such as simplicity, generality, fecundity, and consistency, then we have good reason to believe in the objects that it posits—all of them with no distinction being made between physical and mathematical objects. But according to Azzouni, this is not a true view of science: scientists expect their posits to have an "epistemic role of their own." This may be seen by "noticing how the actual objects under study play an official role in the evidence that epistemic processes are reliable or dependable; in light of this role, scientists are willing to describe such processes as leading to knowledge."[11] For example, suppose that physicists posit a new subatomic particle in order to make a certain group theoretic model apply to their data. Even if their theory very satisfactorily explains their data, typically they will refrain from affirming the existence of the posited particle until they have experimentally detected it. They will require observational evidence that they take to be a reliable indicator of the particle in question. Moreover, in explaining why the evidence reliably indicates the presence of the particle they will ascribe a role to the particle itself in the interactions producing the evidence. It seems then that the holist account of science, at least as expounded by Quine, is inaccurate. And if this is so, then it is reasonable to doubt its application to mathematical knowledge.

Now I think that Azzouni is right that the account of science that he attributes to Quine is not accurate. It is not clear whether this really is Quine's account, since in some of his latter writings Quine retreats from the strong holist theses he advocated in his earlier papers. In any case, if we modify holism, as I have, by distinguishing between local and global conceptions of evidence, then positing in the empirical sciences poses no problems. Empirical scientists are operating with a local conception of evidence which requires them to detect their posits; mathematicians are not.[12]

"Yes," one might object, "but it is exactly because mathematicians are not obligated to detect their posits that mathematical objects are not independent of us." To assess this claim, let us distinguish ontological independence from epistemic independence.[13] An entity is ontologically independent of us if it is not something that we make up, create, or construct, etc.; that is, if it could or would exist even if we did not. From physics itself we know that subatomic particles and other unobservable objects are ontologically independent of us, since physics tells us that they (and the universe they inhabit) existed before we did and would have existed even if we had not. However, mathematics proper, being silent about the nature of its objects, simply does not address the question of their ontological independence. Rather it is philosophers, such as myself, who argue for their ontological independence by arguing that only an ontology of abstract entities can verify the existential claims of mathematics. Those offering the objection opening this paragraph think that unless we can show these abstract entities are epistemically independent of us, we should not accept this philosophical argument for the ontological independence of mathematical objects.

Now a major problem with this objection is that it is very difficult to characterize epistemic independence in a reasonably precise way that doesn't beg the question at issue or classify physical objects as epistemically dependent upon us. To illustrate this, I shall examine the following proposal by Azzouni:

> A requirement of our taking an object O to be [epistemically] independent of us is that, given any property attributed to O, we take ourselves as required to explain how we confirm that attribution in a way that non-trivially satisfies (*). Trivial satisfaction of (*), or the irrelevance of (*) altogether from knowledge-gathering practices about O, indicates that O is [epistemically] dependent on us. [14]

The condition (*) to which Azzouni refers is the following:

> (*) The process by which I come to believe claims about x's is dependable with respect to x's if and only if given that the process has led me to believe $S(x)$ is true, then (under a broad range of circumstances) $S(x)$ must be true, and/or given that the process has led me to believe $S(x)$ is false, then (under a broad range of circumstances) $S(x)$ must be false. [15]

In other words, on this proposal, an object is epistemically independent of us only if: 1) given any property that we attribute to it, we should ordinarily be able to determine by dependable methods whether the property in question applies to that object, and 2) there is a "non-trivial" explanation of why our methods are dependable. [16]

In expounding (*) Azzouni writes that in the empirical sciences, "processes which are taken to yield knowledge are seen as doing so precisely because they do (causally) connect us to objects in such a way that what the process gives as an answer covaries with the properties that the objects have." [17] Later he remarks, "Empirical scientific practice routinely worries about when measurements, observations, and instrumental interventions (with objects) can be trusted and when not; when artifacts of our epistemic means of access arise (and how we can recognize them)."[18] Here he is talking about the dependability of quite specific scientific procedures or instruments. Their analogs in mathematics are algorithms, rules of thumb, estimation methods and approximation procedures; mathematicians do worry about the dependability of these things. Of course, they address their worries by taking some body of mathematics for granted and using that to demonstrate that the method in question is sound or sound for a significant number of examples. Accepted mathematics serves both as the source of data by which the methods are assessed and the background theory used to account for their virtues and foibles.

In both the mathematical and empirical cases one probes or checks or justifies a method, instrument, or datum by reference to a supposedly independent standard. Without such a standard it would be pointless to wonder about the reliability of the items in question. Thus we can calibrate a spring scale by weighing objects of known weights, and we can explain how it registers in response to the forces the objects placed upon it generate. But in order to do this we must assume that we have an independent and accurate method for determining the weights of the known objects, and that our theory of the scale is correct. Even when we give an object an epistemic role, doing so is relative to taking some parts of some theory of objects of that type for granted. When we use a telescope to confirm the existence of a planet originally posited to explain perturbations in the orbit of another planet, we presuppose a theory that permits us to conclude that what we are seeing through the telescope is a planet with sufficient mass to do the work. Thus it seems that both mathematicians and empirical scientists are concerned with issues of dependability and use similar means for addressing them.

What happens when we don't have an appropriately independent theory of the objects in question? According to Azzouni, if we simply say, for example, that our theory of the objects states that our methods for investigating them are dependable, then they are not epistemically independent of us—at least not yet—and we are not justified in asserting their ontological independence.[19] This threatens to undercut the epistemic independence of mathematical objects. We can explain the dependability of, say, our algorithms for calculating sums and products of numbers written in decimal notation by appealing to the recursive equations for addition and multiplication and definitions relating decimal numerals to unary numerals. We might explain the dependability of the former by defining numbers in terms of sets, but obviously the process has to end with assumptions that we cannot independently verify. Affirming that these assumptions are simply stipulated to be true will play right into Azzouni's hand, since the only explanation we will have at this point will be the "trivial" one that the methods are dependable simply because they are (according to our theory of them).

Notice that Azzouni writes that a "requirement of our taking an object O to be [epistemically] independent of us is that, given any property attributed to O, we take ourselves as required to explain how we confirm that attribution in a way that non-trivially satisfies (*)."[20] The same requirement would hold for those who are realists about sub-atomic particles. But this seems to be too much to ask even when we consider relatively familiar objects like electrons, whose epistemic role certainly Azzouni acknowledges. The problem is that we sometimes use purely theoretical considerations to attribute properties to electrons that, as a matter of principle, we can't confirm experimentally. For example, electrons have the property of never being in a state in which they have an exact position and an exact momentum. My limited reading in the philosophy of quantum mechanics tells me that a number of theoretical considerations are needed to conclude that this is an objective feature of electrons and not just a limitation of our measuring devices. If so, then it would seem that in principle we cannot confirm this property of electrons by means of a process that satisfies (*). It may well be the case then that the only way we can confirm it, if at all, is by appealing to some well-confirmed scientific theory. Another example that comes to mind is the continuity of space-time, which seems experimentally indistinguishable from its density.[21]

Now if I am right about these examples, the process scientists have used here seems to be this: To confirm claims about physical objects, which cannot be tested directly by experiments, find a well-confirmed theory (in the usual sense) that implies the claim in question. Demanding that we explain why this process is dependable seems to be demanding too much: it is to demand that we explain why a well-confirmed empirical theory asserts the truth. Suppose that in the light of this, we conclude then that sometimes we are not obliged to explain how we can confirm a property of certain physical objects "in a way that nontrivially satisfies (*)." Isn't this to conclude that (*) is irrelevant in these cases? Now we cannot conclude from this that Azzouni is forced to hold that these objects aren't ontologically or epistemically independent of us. For he only says, "the irrelevance of (*) altogether from our knowledge-gathering practices about O indicates that O is [epistemically] dependent on us...."[22] But it looks like this amounts to his acknowledging that when as a matter of principle (*) is irrelevant, we don't have to try to explain why our practices satisfy it. At most we need only explain why they fail to satisfy it.

This does not seem so different from the case of mathematics. Sometimes we raise issues of reliability and address them by citing accepted mathematical theories. Sometimes we don't raise considerations of reliability and simply depend upon the theory itself eventually being 'confirmed'. Moreover, in these cases, we are typically in a position to explain why we cannot apply Azzouni's criterion (*). The difference between mathematics and physics seems more a matter of degree than of kind with independent confirmation of our physical posits being more readily found and more frequently sought.

The difficulties we have found with Azzouni's proposal generalize to the type of position it reflects. This is the type of position that presupposes that we can access reality independently of our conceptual system. The problem is that our only access to any independent reality is through our sensations. Anything else that we access through them is mediated by hypotheses connecting the two. Walking through the woods during the fall I often smell an odor familiar from my medicine cabinet and infer that there must be some witch hazel nearby. My inference is based upon hypotheses linking the smell and the shrub, which I have conjectured but have never independently confirmed. Of course, with enough effort and care, I could test my hypotheses, but only through taking similar hypotheses for granted. Thus one of the first things I would try is to locate a specimen and smell it, but to do that I would need to (assume that I) know what witch hazel looks like. Most everyday physical objects are capable of affecting each of our five senses, and this provides us multiple ways of independently accessing them. And even when something affects only one or two senses—like the sun—we can often access it from multiple locations and at different times. All this confirms our belief that some enduring object is responsible for the sensations we have on these occasions. But each confirmation is relative to taking for granted myriad hypotheses connecting the object we posit and our sensations. Yet even in mathematics we can find independent links to the various structures it studies. Thus, we use numbers to count sheep, measure the length of a field, register the place of competitors in a race, and determine the iterations of an operation. These different empirical routes to the natural numbers give rise to different mathematical models (for example, set theoretic versus geometric models) of the natural number sequence; and they lend credence to the idea that we are dealing with an independent reality. Again the difference between mathematics and empirical science seems to be a matter of degree.

To quote Quine, "everything to which we concede existence is a posit from the standpoint of a description of the theory-building process." We should add that anything we succeed in accessing we do so only by positing links between them and things whose accessibility we take for granted. Once we realize this, the idea that we can come to know things about patterns through their instances or about types through their tokens becomes much more palatable. As I noted earlier, on the sort of view of mathematical objects I advocate, this does give some mathematical objects an epistemic role.

Clearly, the things we (saints aside) believe in the most are the ones most intimately connected to our senses. We find it harder to doubt that we are standing on firm ground than that the prime numbers go on without end. This may be behind the philosophical intuition that mathematical objects don't exist. Rather than concede to the intuition, I acknowledge that our evidence for mathematical objects is less compelling than it is for everyday material bodies, but I deny that we don't have sufficient evidence for the former. I also deny that we have stronger evidence for any physical object to which we have forged some observational connection than we have for any mathematical object. We have "detected" quarks, but I find it a stretch to say that our justification for believing in them is stronger than our justification for believing in numbers.

Where does this leave us? Some philosophers worry that holding that we posit mathematical objects is incompatible with realism. To them mathematical posits smack more of fiction than of empirical science. Perhaps, they came to this view through overlooking my claim that positing mathematical objects does not guarantee their existence and is only an initial step towards obtaining knowledge of the objects posited. In any case, they are likely to argue their point by emphasizing that mathematicians don't even try to detect their posits whereas empirical scientists normally do. Thus empirical scientists meet their obligations towards an independent reality while mathematicians don't. To this I have responded that the role of mathematical objects does not require them to be detectable; the local conception of mathematical evidence does not admit a place for detecting them. The real question is whether we can get "independent" evidence for a set of axioms, and sometimes we can by modeling them in some previously accepted domain. This is something that mathematicians prize.

As Azzouni pointed out, we cannot explain the reliability of mathematical methods in terms of the mathematical objects themselves, whereas in empirical science we regularly account for the reliability of methods by assigning roles to the objects the methods concern. This is evidence of an independent domain. However, we should not overlook the effort mathematicians devote to establishing the soundness of their methods even if in so doing they don't give a role to individual mathematical objects. Moreover, through positing links between structures and their empirical instances, we can bring mathematical objects into the epistemic picture.

In concluding let me note that my defense of the combination of postulationalism and realism turned little upon structuralism or holism. Structuralism played a part in my response to the Epistemic Role Puzzle, but I think it would have been enough for me to say that mathematics concerns itself with only the structural features of its objects whether they are positions in structures or not. Holism occurred in my account of how we might confirm mathematical posits, but the important point that we can support them using the mathematician's (local) conception of evidence should be separable from my more global conception of evidence.[23] φ

Notes

[1] Quine, W.V., *Word and Object* (Cambridge: MIT Press, 1960), 22.

[2] For a fuller exposition of alternative versions of structuralism, as well as a brief account of its history, see Shapiro, Stewart, *Philosophy of Mathematics: Structure and Ontology* (New York: Oxford University Press, 1997).

[3] Benacerraf's papers are reprinted in eds. Paul Benacerraf and Hilary Putnam, *Philosophy of Mathematics*, 2nd ed. (Cambridge: Cambridge University Press, 1993), 272-294, 403-420.

[4] From the mathematical point of view any infinite progression of sets will serve for defining the numbers. Thus Zermelo defined them as follows: $0 = \emptyset$ (the empty set) $1 = \{\emptyset\}$, $2 = \{\{\emptyset\}\}$, $3 = \{\{\{\emptyset\}\}\}$, and so on. Von Neumann defined them alternatively as follows: $0 = \emptyset$, $1 = \{\emptyset\}$, $2 = \{\emptyset, \{\emptyset\}\} = \{0, 1\}$, $3 = \{\emptyset, \{\emptyset\}, \{\emptyset, \{\emptyset\}\}\} = \{0, 1, 2\}$, and so on. Another famous definition due to Frege and used by Russell defines 0 as $\{\emptyset\}$, 1 as the class of all unit classes, two as the class of all pairs, and so on. There are infinitely many variations on each of these themes.

[5] "What numbers could not be," in Benacerraf and Putnam, p. 294.

[6] I believe the thinking I have outlined in this paragraph was quite common 30 years ago. Today ways of resisting it are on the market, but surveying them would take us too far afield.

[7] For more on my structuralist view, see my *Mathematics as a Science of Patterns* (Oxford: Clarendon Press, 1997).

[8] Azzouni, Jody, "Stipulation, Logic and Ontological Independence," *Philosophia Mathematica*, Series III, vol. 8 (2000): 225-243, 232. See also his *Deflating Existential Consequence* (Oxford: Oxford University Press, 2004) and his "Review of Michael D. Resnik's *Mathematics as a Science of Patterns*," *Journal of Symbolic Logic*, vol. 64 (1999): 922-3.

[9] "Stipulation, Logic, and Ontological Independence," p. 226.

[10] *Deflating Existential Consequence*, p. 109.

[11] "Stipulation, Logic and Ontological Independence," p. 227.

[12] For further discussion, see my *Mathematics as a Science of Patterns*, ch. 7, and my "Quine and the Web of Belief," in ed. Shapiro, Stewart, *The Oxford Handbook of Philosophy of Mathematics and Philosophy of Logic* (New York: Oxford University Press, 2004).

[13] Azzouni does not draw this distinction. For him, epistemic independence is a necessary condition for ontological independence.

[14] "Stipulation, Logic and Ontological Independence," p. 230. Azzouni uses the term "ontological independence" instead of "epistemic independence" in this passage. See the previous note.

[15] Ibid. p. 227.

[16] According to Azzouni, the trivial explanation is this: A process P is reliable with respect to x's because they have the property that P is reliable with respect to them. *Deflating Existential Consequence*, p. 100.

[17] "Stipulation, Logic and Ontological Independence," p. 228, his emphasis.

[18] Ibid. p. 229.

[19] This is because we have given the trivial explanation.

[20] "Stipulation, Logic and Ontological Independence," p. 230, my emphasis.

[21] Another exception to Azzouni's requirement may be properties of objects that are true of them "by definition" such as an electron's property of having one unit of negative charge.

[22] "Stipulation, Logic and Ontological Independence," p. 230, my emphasis.

[23] I am grateful to Kenneth Walden for comments and encouragement. This paper grew out of a paper of the same title that I delivered in December 1999 at a symposium with Jerrold Katz and Stewart Shapiro on the philosophy of mathematics at the annual meeting of the Eastern Division of the American Philosophical Association.

Parfit On What's Wrong

By Thomas W. Pogge

THIS PAPER COMMENTS ON DEREK PARFIT'S SECOND AND THIRD TANNER Lectures,[1] in which he discusses a dazzling array of moral formulas. Parfit treats these as competing formulas. But before we can appreciate his claims about winners and losers, we must first understand what this competition is about: What role are all these formulas meant to play? By reference to which task are we to judge their success or failure?

All formulas canvassed by Parfit substantially involve the noun or verb "act." In the second Lecture, most of the formulas also involve the adjective "wrong." Here, most formulas are criteria for judging which acts are wrong or not wrong, or about how it is wrong or not wrong to act. In the third Lecture, most of the formulas also involve the verb "ought." Here most formulas are criteria for judging which acts one ought or ought not to perform, about how one ought or ought not to act. Because Parfit does not say otherwise, we should assume that he takes the noun and verb phrasings involving "act" to be equivalent, and that he also takes "ought not" and "wrong"—and (one might add) "impermissible"—as coextensive binary predicates. An act is wrong just in case it is impermissible and just in case one ought not to perform it. And one ought to perform an act just in case it is wrong or impermissible not to perform it. We see this presupposed coextensiveness at work when Parfit tells us (338-9) that the Formula of Universally Willed Moral Beliefs (Formula 12)—"An act is wrong unless everyone could rationally will it to be true that everyone believes such acts to be permissible" (338)—can be restated as Kant's Contractualist Formula—"We ought to act on the

Since receiving his Ph.D. in philosophy from Harvard, Thomas W. Pogge has been teaching moral and political philosophy at Columbia University. His recent publications include World Poverty and Human Rights, Global Justice *(edited), "What We Can Reasonably Reject" (*NOÛS 2001*), "Can the Capability Approach be Justified?" (*Philosophical Topics 2002*), and "On the Site of Distributive Justice" (*Philosophy and Public Affairs 2000*). Pogge is editor for social and political philosophy for the* Stanford Encyclopedia of Philosophy *and a member of the Norwegian Academy of Science. His work was supported, most recently, by the MacArthur Foundation, the Princeton Institute for Advanced Study, All Souls College, Oxford, and the National Institutes of Health. He is currently a research fellow at the Center for Applied Philosophy and Public Ethics (CAPPE) at Australian National University, Canberra.*

principles whose universal acceptance everyone could rationally will"
(339). In making this assertion of equivalence, Parfit is surely assuming
that the formulations "an act is wrong unless..." and "we ought to act..."
are both leading up to identifying a property of acts whose absence
makes it the case that the act is wrong and ought not to be performed.

The formulas Parfit canvasses clearly tell us something about
when an act is wrong, is impermissible, or ought not to be performed. It
is less clear whether they also tell us when an act is not-wrong (that is,
right). The fact that an act lacks a property whose presence would make
it wrong is compatible with this act being wrong in some other way.
Even where the formulas Parfit presents are ambiguous on this point,
his discussion makes clear, I believe, that he takes the formulas to give
sufficient and necessary conditions for the wrongness of acts. So I read
all the formulas canvassed as complete (in this sense) criteria for the
wrongness of acts.

Acts here are by Parfit understood as act tokens, such as
particular movements a person intentionally performs, or intentionally
fails to perform, with her body at some particular time and place. It is
notorious that, before acts can be judged by any of the formulas, they
must be individuated. If we do not know how to do this, then we do not
know how to apply any of the competing candidate criteria.[2] But, since
none of the canvassed candidate criteria provides any hint as to how to
solve this problem and since Parfit says nothing about it either, I will
skip it here and pretend that acts are clearly and uncontroversially
individuated for us.

All the candidate criteria Parfit canvasses judge act tokens on
the basis of some type they belong to. This poses another notorious
problem: under what description(s) is a given act to be judged? Just as
one given act type may be instantiated in indefinitely many act tokens,
so one given act token may instantiate indefinitely many act types. In
order to judge a token by its type we thus need to know which type. We
must be able to identify correctly the type or types on the basis of which
the given token is to be judged. The problem is clear when one looks at
the thirteen candidate criteria Parfit distinguishes in his diagram (336).
All these formulas involve references to people acting in this way, or to
what people believe about the permissibility of such acts. All these
criteria are therefore quite meaningless unless we have additional
instructions about how to identify the types that are to inform our
judgment about the act tokens under examination.

To get a taste of the difficulty, consider Parfit's examination of
Formula 11: "An act is wrong unless everyone could rationally will that
everyone acts in this way" (337). Parfit quickly dismisses this formula
by pointing out that "Kant did not act wrongly...in having no children"
(337). But this seems too quick. Let us grant that not everyone can
rationally will that everyone act on the maxim of remaining childless
irrespective of circumstances. But does it thereby forbid Kant's
childlessness? This does not follow, because it is presumably also true

that everyone can rationally will that everyone act on the maxim of remaining childless whenever this is his or her preference and the human population is either large or increasing. In order to tell whether Formula 11 does or does not forbid Kant's childlessness, we must first know which type instantiated by Kant's conduct is the relevant type, referred to by "in this way." Parfit proceeds as if he has an answer to this question, but he does not tell us what this answer is nor, more importantly, how he identified this right answer from among indefinitely many possibilities.

Looking through the whole text, we find some formulas that address this problem. Four distinct approaches are exemplified, though Parfit seems unaware of the distinction. Approach One invokes the descriptions under which the agent herself is intentionally acting. Thus, one of the formulas (named RLN) states that an act is wrong unless the agent could rationally will that everyone does whatever, in acting in this way, she would be intentionally doing (328). To make this formulation mean anything, more needs to be said. In performing some particular act, agents often have several aims in mind as things they are trying to achieve or trying to avoid. Are all these aims relevant, or are further instructions forthcoming about how this list of aims is to be whittled down? And once we have identified the relevant aims: for the act to escape wrongness, must the agent be able rationally to will that all her intentional aims be pursued by everyone, that at least one of her aims be pursued by everyone, that everyone pursue at least one of her aims, or what?

Parfit takes Approach One to be Kant's. But Kant had something quite different in mind when he made the notion of a maxim central to his moral philosophy. I have written elsewhere about Kant's view and should not restate my reading here.[3] But perhaps four short paragraphs are in order to bring out one main contrast between Parfit's reading of Kant and mine.[4]

Parfit seeks a criterion for the wrongness of act tokens which invokes a criterion for the assessment of act types in some subsidiary role. Parfit believes that Kant is pursuing the same project. But this is not so. When Kant formulates the Categorical Imperative, he is not interested in Parfit's problem: the moral assessment of act tokens. Rather, Kant is interested in the moral assessment of act types or, more precisely, of agents' maxims. The Categorical Imperative is a criterion for the permissibility of maxims, and Kant intends this criterion to play a subsidiary role in the assessment of character ("good will")—not in the assessment of act tokens.

In addition, Parfit mistakenly assumes that maxims in Kant's sense are intermediate moral principles. Witness what Parfit calls Kant's Contractualist Formula (339, cited above). The formulas Kant provides do not deal in intermediate moral principles pronouncing on the wrongness or permissibility of act tokens. Instead, they deal in maxims, which Kant defines as subjective principles of volition or of action—that is, as personal-conduct-guiding policies.[5]

So, when Kant says that it is wrong, or rather that we ought not, to act on a certain maxim, he means that it is wrong to have and wrong to act on (remain committed to) this (impermissible) maxim. From this it does not follow that each act performed pursuant to this maxim is wrong. Parfit is quite right to say (297-8) that a gangster is not performing a wrong act when he pays for his coffee merely because doing so is less trouble than stealing it. But this is no criticism of Kant. For when Kant holds that such a gangster acts wrongly he means not that her act (token) is wrong but that her maxim, and her acting on this maxim, is. In fact, Kant offers the shopkeeper example[6] to make just the point Parfit is making with his gangster example. When maximizing her profits by dealing honestly even with inexperienced customers, the shopkeeper is acting according to duty: her act tokens are permissible and so she is not acting wrongly in Parfit's sense. But the shopkeeper fails to act from duty: she is acting wrongly in Kant's sense (in violation of the Categorical Imperative), because it is impermissible to act on the maxim of unconstrained profit maximization. The shopkeeper and gangster cases illustrate Kant's point that conduct can be both right (token) and wrong (type)—that an agent performing permissible act tokens may be acting rightly or wrongly in Kant's sense, depending on the actual maxim of her conduct.[7]

To be sure, Kant held beliefs not only about his questions: "When is a maxim morally wrong?" and "When does a person have a good will?", but also about Parfit's question: "When is an act token morally wrong?" But Kant does not provide a clear path from the first to the last question. The path cannot be this: an act token is morally wrong just in case it is performed on an impermissible maxim. The shopkeeper and gangster examples refute this. The path must be something like this: an act token is wrong (contrary to duty) just in case any maxim on which it might be performed is impermissible.[8] Let us call this Approach Two. None of the criteria Parfit considers is of this kind. But my interest here is in Parfit, not Kant. So I will not try to develop Kant's answer to Parfit's question about when act tokens are wrong.

Ending the digression, let us proceed to the next approach to judging act tokens through a criterion that invokes a subsidiary criterion for the assessment of act types. This approach affects the binary sorting of act tokens via a binary sorting not of act descriptions, nor of maxims, but of intermediate moral principles.[9] Each such moral principle defines a certain type of act and then declares such acts to be right or to be wrong. Of course, there are indefinitely many such principles, often mutually inconsistent. Intermediate moral principles can nonetheless help us achieve a binary sorting of act tokens, provided two conditions are satisfied:

1.   We can tell of at least some of the intermediate moral principles that they are valid.

2.   The set of valid intermediate moral principles is consistent, so that no act token is judged wrong by one valid principle and also judged right by another valid principle.

If the binary sorting is to extend to all act tokens, then a third condition must be satisfied:

3.   For each act token, there is at least one intermediate moral principle that is both known to be valid and applicable to that act token (entailing either that it is wrong or that it is right).

Needed for this approach to work is a subsidiary criterion for judging the validity of intermediate moral principles. The formulas Parfit canvasses in his third Lecture are meant to fulfill this role. It is worth noting that when he discusses any candidate formula for this role, he ignores the question of whether this formula satisfies both conditions 2 and 3.

Yet Parfit may nonetheless be addressing this question indirectly. For many of the formulas he considers speak of 'principles' in the plural. One candidate formula, for instance, declares valid "the principles whose universal acceptance everyone could rationally choose" (361). This formulation is ambiguous between a distributive and a collective use of the plural, and the present approach thus splits into two. Approach Three embraces the distributive interpretation: each intermediate moral principle is tested individually and independently from the others to determine its rational choosability. The winning principles are then conjoined into a set about which one must ask whether it satisfies conditions 2 and 3. Approach Four embraces the collective interpretation: whole candidate sets of intermediate moral principles are tested for rational choosability.[10] Here one might well lay down from the start that a set of principles is rationally choosable only if it satisfies condition 2 and perhaps 3 as well. We may call any set of intermediate moral principles that satisfies 2 a moral code and any set of such principles that satisfies 2 and 3 a complete moral code.

Approach Three runs into a great problem: it is very hard to show that all winning principles are mutually consistent (condition 2) and form a complete set (condition 3). Approach Four also runs into great problems: moral codes are most unwieldy entities—quite tedious to specify in detail and also quite difficult to assess (for rational choosability or whatever determines their validity). Moreover, there is also the problem of uniqueness. It seems highly unlikely that there should be only a single rationally choosable moral code. And this may spell trouble when persons who adopt different valid codes interact in the same world. The fact that each valid moral code is internally consistent does not guarantee that valid moral codes are mutually harmonious.

But perhaps this problem with Approach Four can be turned to advantage. Consider how Parfit criticizes Kant for giving the wrong answer on tyrannicide—holding that, pace Kant, it would have been permissible to assassinate Hitler during the Second World War (321). To be sure, had all Germans believed this to be permissible, Hitler would have been on his guard—no assassination attempt would have succeeded and the Nazis would have been an even greater menace. But Parfit declares this fact irrelevant. He is thereby assuming, in effect, that it is bad if all Germans take tyrannicide to be impermissible, that it is even worse if they all take tyrannicide to be permissible, and that it is best if tyrannicide is taken to be impermissible by a great majority and taken to be permissible by a small clever minority. But how can a morality deliver this result? How can one morality tell its adherents different things about what they may and must not do in identical circumstances? Parfit gives no formula that even attempts to solve this problem which he deems fatal to Kant's view. The trick might be accomplished by a move Parfit does not consider. This move builds on Approach Four in that relevant types of acts are defined by intermediate moral principles which are assessed collectively, as moral codes. The innovation is to construct formulas whose instruction to the agent about which moral code she should follow involves essential reference to the moral codes of other agents. This innovation replicates the conditionalization move I made earlier to defend Kant's childlessness against condemnation by Formula 11. Just as Kant might have acted from a maxim that makes his preferred childlessness conditional upon the actual maxims and conduct of others, so a plausible criterion of wrongness might permit a German to follow a moral code permitting Hitler's assassination just in case the vast majority of Germans follow a moral code forbidding Hitler's assassination.

I lack the space to present or defend a formula that exemplifies this variant of Approach Four. But it deserves study, I believe. It is important that persons choose different professions. So the question, "Which profession is it best for everyone to choose?" starts us off in the wrong direction. If it is desirable that agents follow diverse moral codes, then the question, "Which moral code should everyone follow?" is similarly misguiding.

Let us take stock. I have identified Parfit's project as that of classifying act tokens as either right (permissible) or wrong (impermissible). After pointing out that Parfit fails to address the individuation of act tokens, I have outlined four distinct approaches to his project. Approach One classifies an act token on the basis of a subsidiary criterion that applies to the descriptions under which the agent is intentionally acting. Approach Two, Kant's, classifies an act token on the basis of a subsidiary criterion that applies to the maxims on which agents might perform this act. Approach Three classifies an act token on the basis of a subsidiary criterion that applies to intermediate moral principles permitting or forbidding this act. Approach Four classifies an act token on the basis of a subsidiary criterion that applies to moral codes permitting or forbidding this act. These four approaches to the classification of act tokens as right or wrong are quite different from one another. To be successful, Parfit's discussion needs to bring out these differences—or so I believe.

I conclude with a final reflection on the question of the range of the sought criterion for sorting act tokens into those that are wrong and those that are not wrong. Is this criterion meant to apply *(a)* to all acts by all agents at all times in all possible worlds, or *(b)* to the acts merely of human beings, or *(c)* only to the acts of human beings living under a just legal order, or *(d)* solely to the acts of humans living under a just legal order in a world whose agents all comply with the same intermediate moral principles—or what?

As far as I can tell, Parfit has not attended to this question and has different answers in mind at different times. (It is interesting to observe that—starting around page 328—his wording of the formulas he considers switches from "it is wrong" type formulations to "our act is wrong" or "we ought to" formulations. The use of the first person plural suggests that Parfit is here beginning to think not in terms of what code any one agent should follow, given the actual conduct of the others, but in terms of what code all agents should follow.) This lack of clarity is unfortunate because the question is of great importance. If the range of a formula is *(d)*, or even *(c)*, then, even if correct, it is of no use in the world we inhabit. In this world, we absolutely need a morality that guides us plausibly to adjust our conduct to existing imperfect social institutions and to the conduct of other agents—those who share our morality, those who follow different moralities, and those who are amoral or immoral. φ

Notes

This paper was first presented at a Rutgers University conference (April 2003) which, honoring Derek Parfit on the occasion of his 60th birthday, was entirely devoted to his Tanner Lectures. Larry Temkin organized this memorable and philosophically very productive event. I have reworked my paper so as to accommodate changes that Parfit has made before the publication of his lectures. In doing so, I have greatly benefited from discussions with Rüdiger Bittner and especially Sam Kerstein.

[1] All page references in simple parentheses are to these lectures, entitled "What We Could Rationally Will," *The Tanner Lectures on Human Values*, vol. XXIV, ed. Grethe Peterson (Salt Lake City: University of Utah Press, 2004), 285-369.
[2] For a brief discussion, see my "What We Can Reasonably Reject," *NOÛS Philosophical Issues*, vol. 11, sec. 2 (2001), 118-147.
[3] Compare my "The Categorical Imperative," in *Grundlegung zur Metaphysik der Sitten*, ed. Otfried Höffe. Ein kooperativer Kommentar (Frankfurt: Vittorio Klostermann, 1989), 172-193. Reprinted with revisions in Kant's *Groundwork of the Metaphysics of Morals*, ed. Paul Guyer (Totowa: Rowman and Littlefield, 1998), 189-213.
[4] There are two other major ways in which my reading is at variance with Parfit's. First, I believe that when Kant stresses the equivalency of his formulas (Kant, Immanuel, *Grundlegung zur Metaphysik der Sitten*, *Preußische Akademieausgabe*, vol. 4, 436), he is

not making an assertion, which can be easily set aside as implausible, but issuing a prescription: The various formulas make distinctive contributions to the clarification and specification of the Categorical Imperative—they gradually enrich its meaning, until at last its full import can be understood. Once fully understood, the Categorical Imperative can then be read back into each of these formulas so as to make them equivalent as Kant demands. Second, I think Parfit departs from Kant by plugging into Kant's formulas his (Parfit's) own account of what one can rationally will or want. (Unlike Kant, Parfit does not distinguish these expressions from each other or indeed from what one "could rationally share" (292, 306), "could rationally consent to" (292-5, 298-301, 312-14, 337-8, 352, 359), "could rationally choose" (293-5, 338, 348ff), "to whose acceptance it would be rational to agree" (339, 348).) This is distorting insofar as Kant—especially in the discussion of his second formula—provides his own elaborate account of what a rational being must will and cannot will. Still, in this brief comment, I want to focus on the merits of Parfit's discussion of the many formulas he considers, not on how Kant's view is different from all of them.

[5] Kant, Immanuel, *Grundlegung zur Metaphysik der Sitten*, cit. note 4, 400n, 420n.

[6] Kant, Immanuel, *Grundlegung zur Metaphysik der Sitten*, cit. note 4, 397. Sam Kerstein has forcefully argued that Kant thinks of the shopkeeper as acting on a permissible maxim. If he were right, I wound need to find other evidence to support against Parfit my claim that Kant understood that a person acting on an impermissible maxim may yet produce permissible act tokens.

[7] Likewise, in remaining childless, Kant himself acted rightly (token) and either rightly or wrongly (type)—for instance, rightly on the maxim "to remain childless whenever this is my preference and the human population is either large or increasing," or wrongly on the maxim "to remain childless irrespective of circumstances."

[8] We see here how very hard it would be to show what Kant, at times, seems to have believed—that all act tokens that involve lying are wrong. To show this, one would have to show the impermissibility of each and every maxim pursuant to which certain lies are to be performed under certain conditions. Many of these indefinitely many possible maxims would not even mention lying.

[9] Parfit associates Rawls with this approach. Rawls did indeed make two brief remarks about "rightness as fairness" in his *A Theory of Justice* (Cambridge: Harvard University Press, 1999), 15, 95f. Such a view was worked out by David A. J. Richards in *A Theory of Reasons for Action* (Oxford: Oxford University Press, 1971). But Rawls repudiated the idea later, for example in his *Justice as Fairness: A Restatement* (Cambridge: Harvard University Press, 2001), 186-8. I should add that Parfit also makes deeply mistaken assumptions about how such a view would work when he writes, "Rawls...tells us to suppose that, when we were choosing moral principles, everyone's main aim would be to promote their own well-being" (342-3). I believe this mistake is due to an isolated reading of section 27 of *A Theory of Justice*, where Rawls is sketching not his own view, but a contractualist justification of average utilitarianism. Rawls's own view is different in that the parties in the original position are given to know that those they represent have three higher-order interests—roughly, to develop and exercise their capacities for a sense of justice and a conception of the good and to be successful in the pursuit of the particular conception of the good they have chosen (whose content is not known in the original position). See Rawls, John, *Political Liberalism* (New York: Columbia University Press, 1996), 74, cf. 19.

[10] While Parfit is—intentionally or inadvertently—ambiguous, Scanlon embraces both possibilities. His book provides exactly two full formulations of his "general criterion of wrongness" See Scanlon, T. M., *What We Owe to Each Other* (Cambridge: Harvard University Press, 1998), 11. The first holds that "an act is wrong if and only if any principle that permitted it would be one that could reasonably be rejected" (ibid., p. 4). Later he states his criterion as "an act is wrong if its performance under the circumstances would be disallowed by any set of principles for the general regulation of behavior that no one could reasonably reject" (ibid., p. 153).

An Irrealist Theory of Self

By Jonardon Ganeri

> A false self in the midst ye plant, and make
>   A world around which seems;
> Blind to the heights beyond, deaf to the sound
>   Of sweet airs breathed from far past Indra's sky
> Dumb to the summons of the true life kept
>   For him who false puts by.
>
> —Edwin Arnold, *The Light of Asia*, Book The Eighth.

> Neither self nor no-self in reality is to be found;
> The Great Sage ruled out the views made of self and of no-self.
>
> —Nāgārjuna, *Ratnāvalī* 2.3

1. Three Versions of the 'No-Self' Thesis

IT HAS BECOME A COMMON-PLACE TO READ THE 'NO-SELF' THEORY OF THE BUDDHIST philosophers as a reductionist account of persons. In *Reasons and Persons*, Derek Parfit himself seemed to endorse the association, having learned of the Buddhist theory from his colleague at All Souls College, Bimal Krishna Matilal.[1] The Buddha's denial that there are real selves metaphysically distinct from continuous streams of psycho-physical constituents lends itself, to be sure, to a reductionist interpretation. I believe, nevertheless, that there are good grounds for scepticism, and I think it is time for scholars of Buddhism to be more cautious about the identification than they have been up until now. Different Buddhist

Jonardon Ganeri is a Reader in Philosophy at the University of Liverpool. He read mathematics at the University of Cambridge and philosophy at the Universities of London and Oxford, and has held visiting positions at the Universities of Chicago and Pennsylvania. His work has been in the treatment of Indian philosophical theory from the perspective of contemporary analytic philosophy. His first book, Semantic Powers, *was on Indian philosophy of language from the seventeenth century, and his second,* Philosophy in Classical India: The Proper Work of Reason, *was on Indian accounts of rationality. He has published widely on topics in Indian logical theory, Indian epistemology and philosophy of mind, and more recently, Indian ethics. He is now working on a book on the themes of truth and concealment.*

schools, not to mention different thinkers within particular schools, have given widely varying philosophical construals of the Buddha's claim about 'no-self', and, while some thinkers and some schools might favor a reductionist reading of the claim, others, I would argue, do not. In this paper, I will examine the theory of persons of one such, the Mādhyamika Buddhist Candrakīrti (circa 600–650 CE). Candrakīrti interpretation of the 'no-self' slogan is, I believe, anti-reductionist but irrealist: persons are not reducible to psycho-physical streams, nor are they real existents distinct from the stream. How is it possible for him to say both these things? Let us see.

I begin by charting the terrain. The language of self—use of personal pronouns, proper names, and so forth—is, apparently, representational; that is to say, it appears to refer to and make claims about entities of a certain kind, claims that are assessable as true or false, and whose truth or falsity is determined by the properties of the entities so referred to. Realism about persons is the thesis that appearances here are not deceptive: the terms in this discourse do indeed refer; moreover, assertions made within the discourse are often true, and when true, they are true because the entities so referred to do indeed have the properties ascribed to them. Reductionism has, historically, been a resource of those who would like to defend realism against a perceived threat of ontological proliferation. Reductionism is the thesis that statements in the disputed discourse, when true, are true because of the truth of statements in another discourse, one whose terms refer to entities whose status is less problematic. A committed naturalist who wants neither to admit persons into his or her primitive ontology nor to write off all talk of persons as unintelligible, finds in the strategy of reduction the hope of a salvage operation: the language of self is derivable (possibly with the help of appropriately constrained 'bridge-laws') from the language of psycho-physical continuants. The motto of reductionism is "Realism at no extra expense!" Parfit expresses his reductionism in terms of a commitment to the impersonal description thesis, the claim that "though persons exist, we could give a complete description of reality without claiming that persons exist."[2]

How might reductionism with regard to some domain of discourse be resisted? Broadly, there are three available anti-reductionist strategies. One is to show that the reducing terms (or their referents) inherit their 'shape' or principle of identity from the terms being reduced. If there were no means to individuate distinct streams of pyscho-physical elements other than with reference to persons, the 'reduction' of the language of self into the language of streams would, though formally adequate, fail to be genuinely reductive. A second strategy is to show that the reducing item fails to do the explanatory work of the item being reduced. This strategy seeks to point out distinctive, perhaps non-causal, explanatory work done by the talk of persons or selves. A third strategy hopes to demonstrate that the language being reduced exhibits an essential feature not present in the reducing language. For instance, the anti-reductionist might seek to show that there is an essentially perspectival and consequently subjective element in our talk of selves not captured within the non-perspectival framework of physical science. These three strategies are respectively exemplified in the anti-reductionist arguments of John Campbell, Richard Sorabji, and Thomas Nagel.

Contra reductionist propaganda, an anti-reductionist is not forced into an endorsement of substance dualism. Resistance, however, does incur a substantive obligation: to give an account of the relationship—let us call it the 'dependence' relationship—between talk of persons or selves and talk of psycho-physical streams. That obligation is acute for the anti-reductionist who wishes still to be a realist about persons, but it exists as well for the anti-reductionist who prefers to assume an irrealist position. There are two paradigms here for irrealism. One concurs with the realist that the language of self is a language of referring terms, and of claims made true by the properties of entities so referred to. Where he or she departs from the realist is in issuing a denial that there are, in fact, entities of the kind in question. This is an 'error theory' of the self: our talk of selves is representational but globally in error. There is nothing in the world for our proper names and personal pronouns to denote, nothing to make the statements about selves true: our discourse about persons is systematically mistaken. Terms like "I" and "you" are *empty* terms (and perhaps we can remain agnostic here about whether the statements in which they occur are all false or all neither-true-nor-false). The other irrealist paradigm rejects the assumption shared by the realist and error-theoretic irrealist, the assumption that the language of self is genuinely representational. Both have been misled by the surface grammar of this language; in fact, statements about persons are not truth-apt at all, nor is their function to refer and make claims about things referred to. What is needed, say these "non-factualist" irrealists about the self, is an explanation of the way we use the language of self freed from the mistaken assumption that it is a species of representational discourse; just as, in the prescriptivist and quasi-realist traditions in ethics, the role of ethical statements is not *to assert* anything but to express a moral attitude and prescribe against specified modes of conduct.[3]

Even from this brief review of the terrain, it is clear that there are three distinct positions that a theorist working under the banner of 'no-self' might strike up. To be sure, he may be a reductionist, in which case the docrine of 'no-self' is a thesis that there is no *sui generis* entity irreducible to a psycho-physical stream. But he could also be an error-theoretic irrealist, in which case he will read the slogan as a strict denial that there is anything to which the representational discourse of self refers; he could be a non-factualist irrealist, opting to deny that the surface grammar of our talk of self is a fair guide to its true function. Each of the three positions is, to some extent, in conflict with the pre-theoretic common-sense view of the self. Of the three, the first, reductionism, is the least revisionary. The reductionist's revolution leaves everything pretty much as it was before, subject to a little ontological spring-cleaning; but it is vulnerable to any of the anti-reductionist strategies outlined above. The error-theorist is more revolutionary, for if the entire language of self rests on a massive mistake, surely in an ideal world it should be set aside altogether. The error theorist owes us an explanation of how such a mistake came to be made, how talk of self can have a utility even if it is so colossally mistaken, to what extent thought and talk about the self can be set aside, and what would be the consequences of doing so. In particular, the error-theorist might favor replacement, the substitution of the language of self with talk only of streams or of entities that are by hypothesis reducible to them. Suppose we define the "language of stream-selves" to be the richest language that is, by hypothesis, reducible to the language of streams. Then Parfit's most recent position, if I have understood it rightly, is a combination of an error-theory about the language of selves with a recommendation that we substitute this language for the language of stream-selves.[4]

The non-factualist owes us an explanation of another kind. If the function of our talk of self is, in spite of appearances, not to talk of selves, then what does it do, and how is it related to the talk of psycho-physical streams? The non-factualist will need to explain the extent to which the intuitive commitment to representationalism can be given up, but will distinguish that question from a further one about the extent to which the language of self, irrealistically construed, can and should be surrendered.

2. Candrakīrti's Sense of Self

Candrakīrti IS A NON-FACTUALIST. HE DENIES THAT PERSONS ARE IDENTICAL TO PSYCHO-physical streams, and he also denies that they are distinct; that is, he rejects both reductionism and substance dualism. He argues that there is a point and a function to the "language of self" which is not to refer to and make claims about selves; that is, he rejects representationalism. He discusses the "dependence" of the notion of self on the psycho-physical streams, and he speculates on the possibility for, and consequences of, the giving up of our pre-theoretic commitment to representationalism in the domain of discourse. The principal textual evidence for these claims comes from chapter 6 of the Introduction to the Middle Way (Madhyamakāvatāra),[5] and from his commentary to chapter 18 of Nāgārjuna's famous Lead Verses on the Middle Way (Mū lamadhyamakakārikā).[6] If we are to establish the exact nature of Candrakīrti's view, it will be worth our while to review the texts with some care.

Candrakīrti cautions against a reading of the 'no-self' doctrine that equates it only with the rejection of the "classical" theory of self as an eternal, substantial, independent entity. That would trivialize the doctrine, whereas in fact its implications are much more profound:

[Let us suppose for the moment that] when the absence of self is understood, [this simply entails] a rejection of this "eternal self." But this [reified concept of an eternally existent self] is not considered to be the basis of the clinging to an "I," and therefore why would the philosophical view of a real, substantial self be supported by understanding the absence of a self [in this manner]? Such a proposition would be marvellous indeed!

[It is as if] someone were to see that a serpent had taken up residence in a hole in the wall of his home. He proceeds to assure himself that there is no elephant in the house, and by doing so, he manages not only to dispose of his fear [for the imaginary elephant], but he also rids himself of any apprehension for the serpent! Indeed, our opponent is strikingly naïve [if he would hold such a position]. (MA 6.140–141; trans. Huntington)

Indeed, the idea that "I" refers to a substantial self is not true even at the level of everyday convention (samvrti-satya). It is not even a self-deception: this false self is but false theory–

A self like this simply does not exist, for it is no more produced than is the son of a barren woman. Moreover, it makes no sense that it should serve as the basis for clinging to an "I": We do not consider it to exist even from the perspective of the [truth of the] screen. (MA 6.122; trans. Huntington)

Against the conception of self as mental substance, Nāgārjuna had already said that "if [the self] were something other than [the psycho-physical stream], it would not be characterizable in their terms" (MK 18.1cd). That is to say, we would not be able to say things like "I am hot," "I am walking," "I am happy." Candrakīrti explains:

If the self were other than the psycho-physical elements, its definition would not mention them. The five psycho-physical elements are defined as bodily form, experiencing, seizing on the specific character of things, shaping one's dispositions, becoming aware of objects. The self imagined as wholly other than the psycho-physical elements, just as consciousness is other than physical form, would require a separate definition. (PP 18, 343–344)

If the self is a substance wholly other than the constituents of the psycho-physical stream, then it will have to be described in terms exclusively appropriate to it, just as the Cartesian dualist describes mind in one set of terms ('thinking', and so forth) and matter in another ('spatial extension', and so forth). What then is the origin of the false conception of the self as a distinct substance?

They who, from fear and by not comprehending the nature of acquisitive reification (upādāya-prajñapti), fail to understand that the self is merely nominal, who have veered away even from the truth of concealment, who are deceived by false thinking (mithyākalpanā) into what is only an apparently good argument (anumānābhasamatra), in their delusion conceive of a self and enunciate a definition.... They who seek freedom consider acquisitive reification to constitute the ground of attachment to self among those who run after error (viparyāsa) and false belief (avidyā). (PP 18, 345)

> Therefore there is no self different from the psycho-physical aggregates, for apart from the aggregates it cannot be established. Nor is it considered to be the cognitive basis for clinging to an "I," which is a part of everyday experience. This philosophical view of a self is unreasonable. Even those who have wandered for eons as animals do not perceive this eternal, unborn [self], yet we can see that they still cling to an "I." On this account, there is no self different from the aggregates. (MA 6. 124–5; trans. Huntington)

The conception of self as a distinct substance is a false theory produced by the reification of the facts about the first-person and the sense of self.

If the 'no-self' doctrine is a rejection of the conception of self as mental substance, it is also and equally a rejection of a conception of self as reducible to the psycho-physical stream, the aggregate of the five skandhas. Against reductionism, Nāgārjuna has already stated that "if the self were identical with the psycho-physical stream a part would be rising and [a part] falling" (MK 18.1 ab; cf. 27.6). Candrakīrti's explanatory comment is that:

> The meaning is that one who thinks that the self is the psycho-physical stream arrives at a self as that which rises up and that which falls away — "a part rising and [a part] falling" — because the psycho-physical stream has a part rising and a part falling. However, this is most undesirable, for it implies the fault that the self is plural (ātmanekatvadosa). (PP 18, 342)

The argument that there would be a *division of subjecthood* if reductionism were true is restated in his further discussion of the topic in MA 6.127–37:

> If the self is the psycho-physical aggregates, then there would have to be a plurality of selves, since there is a plurality of aggregates. (MA 6.127 ab; trans. Huntington)

The Buddha, it is true, spoke of the self as the aggregates, but that was only in order to counter the false view that the self is something other than the aggregates (MA 6.132), and in fact:

> The self is similar to a carriage, and the quality of being a carriage derives from the assembled composite of its parts. However, in the sūtras it is said that the self is merely dependent on the aggregates, and on this account the self is not to be directly equated with the composite of the aggregates. (MA 6.135; trans. Huntington)

Candrakīrti's reason for distancing the Buddhist texts from a reductionist account of self is that he does not regard this account as giving a proper analysis of the ordinary concept of self; the latter, he will say, is best analysed in terms of the notion of "appropriation" (upādāna), and:

> It is inherently unreasonable that the appropriator and the appropriated substratum are identical, for if this were the case, then the 'object of action' and the 'agent' would be identical as well. (MA 6.137 ab; trans. Huntington)

If the self is reducible to the psychophysical elements, then no distinction can be made out between the activity of appropriating, and the things appropriated; but our conventional conception of self is precisely that which appropriates the psychophysical elements to itself.

   If the first-person does not refer either to a distinct mental substance or to the psycho-physical aggregate, what alternative is left? In fact, there is a perfectly adequate way to explain how the first-person is used and in what our everyday conception of ourselves consists without the hypostatization and reification of self: one's sense of self consists in the appropriation of psycho-physical elements to oneself. Candrakīrti argues against any representationalist construal of the language of self:

> Consequently, the basis of clinging to an "I" is not an entity. It is not different from the psycho-physical aggregates, it is not the essence of the aggregates, it is not the receptacle of the aggregates, and it does not possess them; [it] is established in dependence on the aggregates. (MA 6.150; trans. Huntington)

In what sense does the concept of self "depend on" the psycho-physical stream, if it is neither reducible to it nor wholly other than it? The leading metaphor for this relationship of dependence is the nature of fire's dependence on fuel. Nāgārjuna again provides the lead, saying, "Everything expounded in terms of fire and fuel is, without exception, applicable to self and the psycho-physical aggregates" (MK 10.15). Candrakīrti comments:

> What the self possesses is what is appropriated (upādāna), namely, the five appropriative factors of personal existence. What is commonly thought of as being based on these factors is the appropriator, the conceiver, the active agent and this is said to be the self. Because the "I-me" sense (ahaṃkāra) is made into an object, the illusion of the "I" is conceived as in and of personal existence. The argumentation concerning the self and what it possesses is to be understood as exactly parallel to that expounded for fire and fuel. (PP 10, 212–213)

This, clearly, is what Candrakīrti considers the everyday conception of self to consist in, an appropriative act of laying claim to the elements in one's own psycho-physical aggregate, an act that does not require there to be any 'entity' or 'object' that is the self, nor any of the usual apparatus of reference to things:

> Because it is taken for granted in the context of everyday experience, we consider the self also to be the appropriator, in dependence on the psycho-physical aggregates, the elements, and the six sense organs with their respective objects. The appropriated substratum is the object of the action, and the [self] is the agent.
> However, because there is no such entity, it is neither eternal nor transitory; it is not produced, nor is it destroyed. It has no quality of permanence and so forth, nor of identity, nor of difference. (MA 6. 162–3; trans. Huntington)

In the *Ratnāvalī,* Nāgārjuna avails himself of another useful metaphor:

> Just as through the medium of (upādāya) a mirror one sees the reflection of
> one's own face, even though it is in fact nothing real, even so one reaches a
> sense of self through the medium of the psycho-physical elements, though in
> truth it is no more real than the reflection of one's face. Just as without the
> medium of a mirror, no reflection of the face can be seen, even so without the
> medium of the psycho-physical elements, there is no sense of self. (R 1.31–3;
> trans. Tucci)

I will continue to explore Candrakīrti's theory of the self conceived of as
an appropriating to itself the constitutents of the psycho-physical
stream—and therefore as 'no-thing'—in the next section. Is it really
possible, though, that the misconstrual of 'I' as referring to some thing
can be eliminated, that we can rid ourself of this self-inflicted self-
deception, of this false self? According to Candrakīrti, it is indeed possible.
His starting point is again a verse from Nāgārjuna's *Ratnāvalī* :

> The psycho-physical complex originated from the sense of self, but this sense
> of self is in reality false (anrta). How can the sprout be true when the seed is
> false? (R 1.29)

Candrakīrti interprets this passage as referring to the conception of 'I' as
an object, and explains that this sense of 'I' is merely an optical illusion;
it is the way the 'I' appears when viewed, as it were, from a distance:

> The sun, at the end of a summer's day when it is throwing out fiery rays of
> light and just as it enters that part of the heavens where there is no cloud, emits
> slanting rays like elongated sparks from a blazing fire and warms the dry earth
> beneath. If one is in the vicinity of this dry area a visual illusion gives rise to
> a mirage which seems to be water. For those at a distance it seems to be clear
> blue water; but for those close by it does not give rise to a mirage.
>   Similarly, for those who are far removed from viewing the nature of self
> and own as they really are, who are caught in the cycle of birth and death, in
> the grip of the misbelief of primal ignorance, for such, a false thing—the self as
> hypostatized on the basis of the skandhas—manifests itself as real. But for
> those close by who see the truth of these matters, no such false thing manifests
> itself. (PP 18, 347; trans. Sprung)

> But linked to this, continuously and strongly, beings cling to 'I', and all that 'I'
> possesses is conceived as 'mine'. This self will manifest empirically, the fruit
> of ignorance, as long as it's not subject to analysis. Without a worker, there's
> no work performed. And likewise without 'I' there is no 'mine'. Perceiving
> that both 'I' and 'mine' are void, the yogī will be utterly free. Vases, canvas,
> bucklers, armies, forests, garlands, trees, houses, chariots, hostelries, and all
> such things that common people designate, dependent on their parts, accept
> as such. For the Buddha did not quarrel with the world. Parts and part-
> possessors, qualities and qualified, desire and those desiring, defined and
> definition, fire and fuel—subjected, like a chariot, to sevenfold analysis are
> shown to be devoid of real existence. Yet, by worldly, everyday convention,
> they exist indeed. (MA 6 164–7; trans. Huntington)

The misconception that 'I' is a referential expression is an illusion which results from standing too far back from the facts of personal identity, namely the psycho-physical stream, just as a cloud or a table looks from a distance like a solid object, but dissolves into vapor or atoms on closer inspection. To put matters another way, the level of description to which this use of 'I' belongs is a level that concerns itself with such matters as the re-identification of persons over time, rather than the level of description at which one is concerned with matters of composition. These two levels of description are not incompatible with one another, but when it comes to settling questions about what there really is in the world, the 'view from close-up' is the proper one to assume. We can certainly agree with Candrakīrti that the world described according to the 'view from close-up' need not share the ontology of the world as described from far-off. What requires further argumentation is the additional claim that the ontology of the 'view from close-up' has a greater claim to *reality* than the ontology of the view from far-off. We do not typically regard clouds and tables as optical illusions simply because they disappear when we 'zoom in'. The same is true of the chariot—why does the possibility of analysis, or the redescription of the chariot in terms of its parts, call into question the reality of the chariot itself, described at the level of wholes? Why should there not be, as philosophers as diverse as Michael Dummett and the Jainas have maintained, different but compatible levels of description, each with its own proper domain of objects? Why should we not say that when we look at an impressionist painting close-up and see only dots of colour, the disappearance of the painting is the illusion and the 'real' painting is the one seen from far-off?

According to the non-factualist, we have simply misunderstood the grammar of 'I' if we think of it as a referring term, rather than a term whose linguistic use is to perform an expressive act of appropriation. Suppose then we rid ourselves of at least this mistake. Can a human person go further and give up the language and concept of self altogether, even understood as having the non-representational use the non-factualist claims it to have? Nāgārjuna:

> Without 'me' or 'mine' because the self and what belongs to it are still, he who is without 'me' or 'mine' does not exist. One who perceives that which is free of 'me' and 'mine' does not perceive. When 'me' and 'mine' are destroyed both within and without, appropriation (upādāna) comes to an end; with its demise, rebirth ends. (MK 18.2 cd – 18.4)

Nāgārjuna's startling claim would appear to be that with the cessation of all use of the vocabulary of self, the person quite literally ceases to exist. Candrakīrti modifies the claim, interpreting it as a shedding of the misconception that there is a permanent substantial self, something that is possible for the adept at a final stage of the Buddhist path. But if all activity of self-appropriation of the psycho-physical is abandoned, then, he too agrees, it is the end:

> This belief in the permanent self is brought to an end by no longer having a sense of self and of what belongs to self. From that sense coming to an end the four kinds of appropriation (upādāna) — to sense pleasure, to dogmas, to morality, and to belief in the permanent self — ceases. From the cessation of appropriation, personal continuity defined as re-birth is ended. The sequence of stages in the cessation of rebirth is like this. Appropriation having ceased, there is no personal continuity. When personal continuity has come to an end, how can there be the cycle of birth, old age and death? (PP 18, 349 on MK 18.5a)

There are two stages in the path from ignorance about the self to transformation of mind. One stage involves the elimination of a false representational conception of self and the language of self, a conception that is to be replaced by an appropriative model of self-knowledge and self-reference. The second stage involves the elimination even of acts of self-appropriation. While the completion of the first stage frees one from egotism and self-interested or self-centered motivation, but leaves one with a residual sense of self and an ability to discriminate between oneself and others, the completion of the second stage is the culmination of a process of complete self-annihilation, self-surrender and loss of autonomy. This is, perhaps, nirvāna, and it is for that reason that the way of the bodhisattva is the way of the first stage alone. The bodhisattva retains a residual sense of self-sufficiency for moral agency and altruistic action. What I shall therefore be interested in is the possibility of a non-vacuous conception of self that is free of the representationalist error — a sense of self without a false self.

3. Of Me and Mine: The Appropriativist Theory of Self
IF I AM RIGHT, Candrakīrti's VIEW IS THAT THE LANGUAGE OF SELF — USE OF WORDS like 'I', 'mine', 'you', and so forth — is not properly understood as having a representational function. This is an illusion of common sense and surface grammar, an illusion which dissolves on close analytical inspection. Giving up this illusion implies much more than merely giving up the idea of a mental substance; it requires surrender even of a reductionist conception of self. But it does not yet follow that there is no explanatory account of the utility of the language of self. What, then, is the use of the language of self? The word 'I' is used, it seems, to perform an appropriative function, to claim possession of, to take something as one's own (compare upādāna: "the act of taking for one's self, appropriating to one's self"). The appropriation in question is to be thought of as an *activity* of laying claim to, not the making of an *assertion* of ownership. When I say, "I am happy," I do not assert ownership of a particular happy experience; rather, I appropriate the experience within a stream, and in doing so lay claim to it. Call this the appropriativist theory of self. It has the virtue of elucidating the relation of dependence

between the language of self and the psycho-physical streams, and it ties in with the sorts of consideration about the grounding of our concept of self that have been brought to the fore by Richard Sorabji.[7] In particular, Sorabji argues that facts of ownership are the 'further facts' not accounted for by a reductionist theory of self. The point of contention between the realist and the irrealist is over whether to give a deflationary or a robust interpretation to the 'further fact' of ownership.

Āryadeva, the younger contemporary of Nāgārjuna and co-founder of Madhyamaka Buddhism, rehearses a curious argument in support of the Buddhist thesis that there are no selves:

> That which is self to you is not self to me; from this fixed rule it follows that it is not self. Indeed, the construction [of self] arises out of the impermanent things. (CS 10.3)

T.R.V. Murti ventures the following paraphrase of this difficult verse:[8]

> If the ātman were a real entity, there should be agreement about it. On the contrary one's (self) ātman is anātman (non-self) for another, and vice versa; and this should not be the case if it were an objective reality.[9]

Murti's paraphrase hints at an interesting reading of the argument in the verse. Why do human beings have a concept of self? What work does it do? Possession of a concept of self is important because it enables me to think of my ideas and emotions, my plans and aspirations, my hopes and fears, as *mine*—as *belonging* to me and the proper objects of my concern. Equally, it is the concept of self which is in play when I think of your ideas and emotions, your plans and aspirations, your hopes and fears, as *yours*—the proper objects of *your* concern. A human being without a concept of self, therefore, would be a seriously impoverished creature. Lacking the concept of self, I would not be able to draw the distinction between what is mine and what is yours, and, unable to make that distinction, I should also lack the capacity to form plans or act on intentions, not to mention the ability to make promises, enter into commitments, or accept responsibility. For example, I could not be in a position to intend to do something, for I would not understand that the intention is fulfilled only if I and nobody else performs the action intended. It is our capacity to make out that distinction to which Āryadeva draws our attention when he says that "that which is self to you is not self to me." What we have here is an adequacy condition on potential theories of self.

It is at this point that Āryadeva's argument takes an interesting turn. What Āryadeva next argues is that the classical theory of self fails the adequacy condition. The classical theory asserts that selves exist as real and permanent entities; it reifies the facts of selfhood, and accounts for our possession of a concept of self on the model of our possession of concepts of external objects. Ārydeva's refutation of the classical theory involves the claim that this is a false model. For our concept of an object is a concept of something public, an inhabitant of a shared world, something that can equally well and simultaneously be the common focus of *your* and *my* attention. To reify the self, to explain our possession of a concept of self on the model of our possession of the concept of an object, is thus precisely to render one incapable of explaining why we have the concept of self in the first place, by sustaining the notion of something being exclusively or distinctively *mine*.

Candrakīrti's commentary on the first half of CS 10.3 strengthens the argument and relates it to the Buddhist theory:

> It follows that the self does not exist essentially (svarūpatah). If the self were to exist essentially, then just as it would be the foundation of one person's sense of 'I', so it would be the foundation of everyone's sense of 'I'. For it is not the case that the essential nature of fire is burning and yet that sometimes it does not burn. So if the self were to exist essentially, it would be the self for everyone and the focal point of their sense of 'I'. And this is not the case, for That which is self to you is not self to me; from this fixed rule it follows that it is not self.

> That which is self to you, the focal point of your sense of 'I' (ahamkāra) and self-concern (ātmasneha), that indeed is not self to me; for it is not the focal point of my sense of 'I' and self-concern. This then is the fixed rule from which it follows that it is not [a real thing]. There is no essence to such a self as is not present invariably. One should give up the superimposition of a self, as being something whose content of which is unreal (asadartha).

This seems to be an inversion of the third type of anti-reductionist argument mentioned above: there are features of the language of self that the realist construal of that language necessarily omits.

4. Body-swapping and Personal Survival

FURTHER DISCUSSION OF THE ARGUMENT, OR AT LEAST A CLOSELY SIMILAR ONE, IS AVAILABLE in the *Mahāprajñāpāramitāsāstra*.[10] I will not follow Étienne Lamotte in endorsing the Chinese tradition's attribution of the text to Nāgārjuna:[11] but whoever is responsible for the original compilation, it remains an important source for early Madhyamaka. The discussion begins with three suggestions as to why a notion of self as distinct from psycho-physical streams is required. The first is that "each individual person conceives the notion of the self in relation to his own person (svakāya), not in relation to that of someone else. If, therefore, he wrongly considers as self the non-self of his own person, he would also wrongly consider as self the non-self of another person" (p. 736). Lamotte reads the argument as an insistence that my concept of myself as distinct from you is explicable only if the concept "corresponds with something real," and regards it as presenting the position refuted in CS 10.3. The second argument is that "if there is no internal self, [being given that] acquaintance with colors arises and perishes from moment to moment, how does one distinguish and recognise the color blue, yellow, red or white?" (p. 736) This looks as if it is an early statement of what was to become a very influential argument in favour of the self, found in the commentaries to *Nyāya-sūtra* 3.1.1, that the self is required by the possibility of psychological unity and the reidentification of objects. Finally, another argument familiar from the *Nyāya-sūtra is* rehearsed, that "if there is no self, and since the knowledge of human activities, arising and perishing repeatedly, all disappear with the life of the body, who then is left to reap the rewards—good or bad? Who endures sadness or happiness? Who is set free?" That echoes the familiar argument of Vātsyāyana in his commentary to *Nyāya-sūtra* 1.1.10.

Our present interest is in the first of these arguments. If the concept of self is grounded in notions of self-concern and a sense of 'I' as distinct from 'you', then the question we need to consider is whether what matters to me when I think about my survival and future well-being is the continuity and status of the stream of psycho-physical events, or whether what matters to me is the future existence and status of a person numerically identical to myself. Derek Parfit famously introduced a science-fiction example to test our intuitions about this question.[12] He asked us to imagine that we are stepping into a teletransporter, a machine that completely destroys the body at the same time as it transmits all the physical and psychological data necessary to reconstitute the person in another transporter remotely situated, and he argues that we care less about the imminent destruction of our old body than about the continuity of our psychological lives in the life of the replica. What about the slightly modified case in which, as a result of a malfunction, my old body is not destroyed but continues to live as before (Parfit calls this the Branch Line case)? Suppose I step out unharmed from the teletransporter, only to to be told that I am about to die. Do the well-being and good prospects of my replica far away (someone who has all my memories and personality traits, and calls himself by my name) provide me with comfort in the face of my imminent death? Here our intuitions are less clear, and for Parfit that is exactly how they should be if our concern tracks the continuity of the stream rather than numerical identity. The relation of numerical identity is definite, relations of psycho-physical continuity indefinite; and if there is an indefiniteness in the object of our self-concern and sense of 'I', then these notions follow continuity relations rather than relations of numerical identity.

The author of the *Mahāprajñāpāramitāsāstra* brilliantly anticipates Parfit here. He claims that there are circumstances in which ambiguity creeps into the notion of self, and he tests our intuitions, not by means of science fiction but with stories taken from the legends. He tells the story of…

> … a man who has been charged with travelling far finds himself spending the night alone in a deserted house. In the middle of the night, a demon carrying on his shoulders a dead man came and put it down in front of him. Then another demon came in pursuit of the first demon, and angrily reproached

him, saying: "That dead man belonged to me—how come it was you who
brought him here?" The first demon replied: "He is my property; it is I who
brought him myself." The second demon responded: "It is in fact I who brought
the dead man here." These two demons, each grasping the dead man by a
hand, argue over him. The first demon says: "Here is someone who we could
interrogate." And the second demon starts to question him and says: "Who
brought the dead man here?" The man comes up with the following reflection:
"These two demons are very strong. If I tell the truth or if I lie, my death is
certain, and in either case I will not be able to avoid it. What good is it to lie?"
He declared therefore that it was the first demon who had brought the dead
man there. At that point, the second demon very angrily seized him by the
hand and tore his hand off and threw it to the ground. But the [first] demon
took a [hand] from the corpse and he fitted it to him. In the same manner, he
substituted in the man's body the two arms, the two feet, the head and the sides
of the corpse. And together the two demons devoured the body of the man
whose body they had substituted with that of the corpse. Then after wiping
their mouths, they left. The man reflected again: "I have seen with my own
eyes those two demons devour completely the body which was born from
my mother and father. Now my present body is entirely made up of the flesh
of another. Have I now a body or have I no longer a body? If I believe I have
one, it is entirely the body of another; if I believe I don't have one, here
nevertheless is a visible body." When he thought about this, his mind was
greatly troubled, and he acted like a man who had lost his reason. The next
morning, he left and set out again. Arriving in a kingdom, he saw in a Buddhist
stupa an assembly of monks, from whom he inquired if his body existed or
not. The monks asked him: "Which person are you?" He replied: "I do not
know if I am a person or if I am not a person." He then told the assembly what
had happened. The monks said: "This man has by himself recognised the non-
existence of the self; he will be saved easily." Addressing him, they said to
him: "Your body, from its origin right up to today, has always been deprived
of self. And that's not just the case now. It's simply because the four great
elements were combined together that you thought 'This is my body'. Between
your past body and the one of today, there is no difference." The monks
converted him to the Path; he severed his ties and became an Arhat.

The moral of this story is three-fold. First, the recognition that I have a
concern for my future survival and a concern for my own well-being, as
distinct from any concern I may have for your survival and well-being,
does not require the postulation of selves as objects ('false' selves). Indeed,
if Āryadeva is right, such a postulation would singularly miss its mark,
trying, as we might put it, to render objective the essence of the subjective.
Second, the preservation of physical continuity is not the only matter of
importance in the question of my survival; psychological continuity
without physical continuity is sometimes enough to assuage a concern
about the future. Third and finally, it is far from certain and definite
whether I attach more weight to my physical continuity or to my
psychological continuity. Both seem important, and cases where they
come apart are extremely vexing (especially if one is the victim of a
body-snatcher). This very indefiniteness supports the view that it is
relations of continuity rather than of strict numerical identity which
are in brought into play in the application of notions of self-concern and
sense of 'I'. The author of the *Mahāprajñāpāramitāsāstra* did not, but easily

could have continued his story by imagining that the demons regurgitated and reconstituted the body of the unfortunate man. In this Ship-of-Theseus scenario, just as in the Branch Line version of the teletransporter, our intuitions become blurred.

5. Āryadeva Again

LET US RETURN NOW TO THE SECOND HALF OF ĀRYADEVA'S ARGUMENT IN *CATUHSATAKA* 10.3. Āryadeva has presented us, in effect, with an adequacy condition on any putative theory of self — that it must be able to explain the possibility and significance of the contrast between mine and yours — and he has argued further that the classical theory of self, which claims that selves are real mental entities, is unable to explain even how that contrast is possible. What then about the Buddhist theory of self itself? How well does it fare? The Buddhist theory, as articulated by Candrakīrti in his comment on the second half of the verse, is that a concept of self is a superimposition onto the aggregate stream of psycho-physical events:

> If there is no self, whence this sense of 'I' and self-concern? Our author says:

> Indeed, the construction [of self] arises out of the impermanent things. Although, from the rule mentioned above it follows an actual self as essential and distinct from the psycho-physical constituents never exists, still a constructed idea of self [arises] out of the impermanent things that do exist– physical attributes, cognitions, sensations, volitions and conceptions (rūpa-vedanā-samjñā-samskāra-vijñāna). A superimposition (kalpanā) is made whose content is unreal (abhūtārtha), that the self exists and lives and moves about. A self is hypostasized (prajñapyate) as dependent on the psycho-physical constituents, just as fire is dependent on kindling. The meaning of the statement that there is a construction of self out of the impermanent elements is that it is constructed by hypostasization dependent on the notion that it does not exist essentially but as different in nature from the constituents and yet determined in a fivefold way.

If it is a mistake to think of a person's identity as consisting in their possession of an essence, it does not follow that we do not have a concept of self and a notion of self-concern. Candrakīrti claims that these notions arise out of and bear upon relations of psycho-physical continuity rather than numerical identity over time. I have concern for the future states of the stream of psycho-physical events that is me, you for yours. The contrast between our respective concerns is made out without resort to the thought that what I am is an entity with a strict identity across times. What Candrakīrti claims, therefore, is that when I express a concern about my future survival or the success or failure of my plans and intentions, what properly sustains my concern is the psycho-physical stream, and not the future condition of a numerically identical self.

A different worry now is that while the Buddhist theory can make sense of the *possibility* of the distinction between mine and yours, it is incapable of sustaining a plausible explanation of the *point* and *significance* of that distinction. Richard Sorabji has recently pressed the objection against both Parfitian and Buddhist accounts of the self.[13] The substitution of our ordinary talk about myself and other persons with talk about this or that stream of psycho-physical events deprives our use of such notions as responsibility, commitment, credit, blame, pity, and compassion, and even intention, shared attention, and social referencing of much of their point. Suppose, for example, that I intend to shout at someone in order to draw their attention to me. Substituting the vocabulary of 'I' and 'they' for talk of this and that stream, we shall have to redescribe the situation as one in one stream contains a desire that another stream 'should' contain an attention produced by the shouting. Here, Sorabji says, the word,

> "should" means that it would be desirable, but we are not supposed to talk of anybody for whom it would be desirable, only of the desirability of one stream containing a shouting and the other a resultant attention, presumably because the total situation with its various streams would be more 'desirable' from a rather abstract point of view. But intention, conceived this way, seems to have lost much of its point and motivation precisely because there is no one for *whom* the outcome would be desirable.

Likewise with credit and blame—we can no longer say that there is a *person* who deserves credit or blame, for "it would be the *act* that deserved credit and blame, and the resulting stream, but in the different sense that it would be more admirable, or less so, just as a sunset may be admirable, without anybody *deserving* credit or blame." The point is that it no longer seems to matter much whether a particular good experience is included in this stream rather than that: "It is better," Sorabji continues,

> that the universe should contain good experiences rather than bad, but as to which stream of consciousness they might enter, why should that matter? Perhaps because it is preferable that experiences should occur in some sequences rather than others, since their significance will be altered by the sequence. But this would only motivate a preference for certain *types* of sequence over others. Detachment would have been achieved, but at rather a high price.

Sorabji's argument is closely related to what Parfit calls the Extreme Claim, the claim that "if the Reductionist View is true, we have no reason to be concerned about our own futures."[14] Ordinarily we think that while knowing that somebody will suffer a pain gives me at least some reason to prevent it, knowing that it is I who will suffer the pain provides an 'additional reason' to act. According to the Extreme Claim, however, a reductionist must deny that there are any such "additional reasons"; thus Parfit: "That some pain will be *mine* does not, in itself, give me any *more* reason to prevent the pain."[15] If this is thought implausible, then perhaps, instead, the fact that the pain will belong to the same psycho-physical stream as the expectation itself provides a reason for special concern: this is what Parfit calls the Moderate Claim.

Parfit acknowledges that the idea that there is a distinction between the concern one has for the pain of another and the *anticipation* of one's own future pain, and that it is hard to see how a reductionist can give weight and importance to that distinction, but declares himself unable to find a conclusive argument for or against either the Extreme or the Moderate Claim. Perhaps we should just give up anticipating our future pains.

Āryadeva, clearly, is sensitive to this worry, and the second half of his argument is an attempt to address it. The objection derives its force from the presumption that talk of this and that stream cannot 'sustain' or 'support' the common use of a vocabulary of me and you, and the whole system of concepts co-implicated with the concept of self, but has rather to be thought of as a substitute for it. But Āryadeva affirms that the popular notion of 'I' is constructed out of the impermanent psycho-physical events, and Candrakīrti explains the relation of dependence between the two vocabularies as akin to the dependence of fire on kindling. Candrakīrti's position is that as long as we are careful to separate the notion of self from any false imputation of ontological commitment to a real mental substance, the residue is a concept of self that can be sustained by talk of this and that psycho-physical stream, and in turn sustains the vital contrast between 'mine' and 'yours'. He is not a reductionist, for he does not claim that the language of self can be translated without loss into the language of psycho-physical streams, any more than talk of the fire is simply talk of the kindling. Nor is his a replacement account, for he does not think either that the use of the vocabulary of mine and yours can be dispensed with entirely, in favour of speaking only about the streams. We need the language of self to make sense of the importance of the distinction between mine and yours, and these are 'further facts' over and above *but not independent of* facts about the streams.

The utility of 'I' consists in its being the means by which appropriation occurs, the taking of something as a distinctive object of concern. An appropriative explanation of the use of 'I' does not require that it have a representative function, and the false if common-sensical idea that there is a real something to which 'I' refers can with effort be given up. Anscombe seems to have a sort of appropriative explanation in mind when she says that the proposition "I am this thing here" is not an identity but a 'subjectless' construction meaning "this think here is the thing of whose action this idea of action is an idea, of whose movements these ideas of movement are ideas, of whose posture this idea of posture is the idea."[16] And Locke seems to be on the same track when he says that we create a self insofar as we *reconcile* and *appropriate* actions (*Essay* 2.27.26), and insofar as our consciousness *joins itself to* and is *concerned for* certain bodily parts (2.27.17-18).

What is still far from clear is whether one could go a step further and give up the appropriative practice while continuing to be a human being in the world. Entirely giving up that system of appropriative concepts would utterly transform one's inner world, in ways we might find almost unintelligible. It is hard even to imagine how the mind of a Buddha might work, and perhaps we should not try. It is interesting, though, to make the comparison with the absolute self-surrender expected of a "revolutionary":

> The revolutionary is a lost man; he has no interests of his own, no cause of his own, no feelings, no habits, no belongings; he does not even have a name. Everything in him is absorbed by a single, exclusive interest, a single thought, a single passion—the revolution. In the very depths of his being, not just in words but in deed, he has broken every tie with the civil order, with the educated world and all laws, conventions and generally accepted conditions, and with the ethics of the world. He will be an implacable enemy of this world, and if he continues to live in it, that will only be so as to destroy it the more effectively…. For him, everything that allows the triumph of the revolution is moral, and everything that stands in its way is immoral.[17]

The enlightened mind is a revolutionary mind, and the Buddha indeed would have us all become revolutionaries in thought, enemies of the conventional world of pain and suffering. And—who knows—perhaps he did also desire quite literally to create a band of revolutionaries that might upturn an unjust and inflexible brahminical social order, manufacturing the revolutionary mind and using religious soteriology as the well-chosen skillful means, the right clothes in which to wrap a concealed truth. Be that as it may, what I have attempted to show is that there is in Buddhism a viable irrealist and non-reductionist analysis of our ordinary conception of self. This unpacking of the deepest roots of our thinking about ourselves and our place in the world is, I hope it will be generally agreed, a philosophical project par excellence. φ

Notes

[1] Parfit, 1984: 273, 502–3. For Matilal, see his 2002.

[2] Parfit, 1984: 212.

[3] A third paradigm for irrealism is, of course, the semantic anti-realism of Michael Dummett; but it is less than clear to me that this paradigm is available in an account of the language of self. Mark Siderits, however, has recently provided an argument for the viability of an anti-realist construal of the language of self, and he is also willing to attribute the construal to the followers of Madhyamaka Buddhism (Siderits 2003). The merits of his "Buddhist anti-realism" require further investigation, as does Roy Perrett's interpretation of Madhyamaka Buddhism as a type of "minimalism" (Perrett 2002).

[4] Parfit, 1999.

[5] The text is now extant only in Tibetan. I will follow the translation of Huntington and Wangchen, 1989. A new translation by Peter Ebbatson is currently under way.

[6] Sprung's translation of Candrakīrti's commentary is dependable; there are several readable translations of Nāgārjuna, of which Garfield 1995, although based on the Tibetan, is arguably the best.

[7] Sorabji, unpublished.

[8] One difficulty relates to the compound ātmāniyamāt. I have followed Candrakīrti in reading ātmā niyamāt "from a fixed rule"; the Tibetan, however, reads ātmā aniyamāt

(ma nes phyir) "from the absence of a fixed rule."
[9] T. R. V. Murti, 1960: 204.
[10] *Le Traité de la Grande Vertu de Sagesse de Nāgārjuna* (*Mahāprañjāpāramitāsāstra*), translated from the Chinese by Étienne Lamotte (Louvain, 1944), volume 2, pp. 736–750. English translation by Anita Ganeri.
[11] In his introduction to volume 3 of the translation, Lamotte withdraws the identification, giving as his grounds a dating of the author of the *Traité* as approximately the beginning of the fourth century A.D. John Brough speculates that the erroneous attribution to Nāgārjuna may have begun with Kumārajīva: "There is no doubt whatsoever that the Chinese translator Kumārajīva believed that the *Traité* was the genuine work of the original Nāgārjuna; and for this belief he had reasonable excuse, since the work is in the main Madhyamaka tradition, and refers to and sometimes paraphrases the Madhyamakakārikās. This being so, it is natural to assume that the attribution of the *Traité* to Nāgārjuna is simply a mistake due to Kumārajīva or his near-contemporaries" (Review of Lamotte, BSOAS, p. 165).
[12] Parfit, 1984, chapter 10.
[13] Richard Sorabji, unpublished.
[14] Parfit, 1984, chapter 14.
[15] Parfit, 1984: 308.
[16] Anscombe, 1991.
[17] From the *Revolutionary Catechism* written by Nechaev and Bakunin in 1869. See Franco Venturi, *Roots of Revolution* (New York: Alfred A. Knopf, 1960), 365–6.

Bibliography

CS   = Āryadeva's Catuhsataka. See Bhattacharya.
CSV = Candrakīrti's Catuhsatakavrtti, a commentary on CS. See Bhattacharya.
MA = Candrakīrti's Madhyamakāvatāra. See Huntington.
MK = Nāgārjuna's Mūlamadhyamakakārikā. See Garfield.
PP = Candrakīrti's Prasannapadā, a commentary on MK. See Sprung.
R = Nāgārjuna's Ratnāvalī. See Tucci.

Anscombe, Elizabeth, "The first person," S. Guttenplan (ed.), *Mind and Language*, (Oxford: Clarendon Press, 1975), *Wolfson College lectures*, repr. in *Collected Philosophical Papers*, vol 2 (Cambridge 1991).
Bhattacharya, Vidhushekhara, *The Catuhsataka of Āryadeva*. Sanskrit and Tibetan Texts with Copious Extracts from the Commentary of Candrakīrti. (Calcutta: Visva-Bharati.)
Campbell, John, *Past, Space, & Self* (Cambridge: MIT Press, 1994).
Duerlinger, James, "Reductionist and Non-reductionist Theories of Persons in Indian Buddhist philosophy," *Journal of Indian Philosophy*, vol. 21 (1993): 79–101.
Garfield, Jay L, *The Fundamental Wisdom of the Middle Way: Nāgārjuna's Mūlamadhyamakakārikā* (New York: Oxford University Press, 1995).
Huntington, C. W. and Geshe Namgyal Wangchen, *The Emptiness of Emptiness* (Honolulu: University of Hawaii Press, 1989).
Locke, John, *An Essay Concerning Human Understanding*, ed. P. Nidditch (Oxford: Clarendon Press, 1975).
Matilal, Bimal Krishna, *Mind, Language and World. Collected Essays*, vol. 1 (Delhi: Oxford University Press, 2002).
Murti T. R. V., *The Central Philosophy of Buddhism: A Study of the Mādhyamika System* (London: Uniwin, 1960).
Nagel, Thomas, "What is it like to be a bat?". repr. in *Mortal Questions*, 1979.
Parfit, Derek, *Reasons and Persons* (Oxford: Clarendon Press, 1984).

Parfit, Derek, "Experiences, subjects and conceptual schemes," *Philosophical Topics*, no. 26 (1999): 217-270.

Perrett, Roy, "Personal identity, minimalism and madhyamaka," *Philosophy East & West*, vol.52, no.3 (2002): 373–385.

Siderits, Mark, *Buddhist Philosophy and Personal Identity: Empty Persons*. Ashgate (2003).

Sorabji, Richard, "Is there a continuous self? Buddhism and its Indian opponents" (unpublished).

Sprung, Mervyn, *Lucid Exposition of the Middle Way: The Essential Chapters from the Prasannapadā of Candrakīrti* (Boulder, Colorado: Prajña Press, 1979).

Tucci, G., "The Ratnāvalī of Nāgārjuna," *Journal of the Royal Asiatic Society* (1934): 307–325; (1936): 237–252, 423–435.

A Mistrustful Animal

An Interview with Bernard Williams

HRP: How did you come to be interested in philosophy?

Williams: It was the old story of getting interested in the subject before I knew that there was such a subject. When I was at school, some friends and I started talking about a set of issues which I would now call 'philosophical'. Some of these issues were political. At that time, we were at war and allied with the Soviet Union, so discussions about communism occupied us. I was also already much occupied by questions having to do with art and morality and the autonomy of the artist. As it happened, my headmaster, who was a fervent Oxford man, sent me in for a scholarship in Classics at Oxford. It was only after I got there that I discovered that the course I had enrolled in—the so-called 'Greats Course'—included philosophy. That was rather nice, since it meant that I was going to be studying the kind of things that already interested me. However, it wasn't that I just wanted to do philosophy and just did some Classics along the way; I was always very interested in Classics.

Bernard Arthur Owen Williams (1929-2003) was a Fellow of All Souls College, Oxford, and taught at Cambridge University, University College London and the University of California, Berkeley. His books include: Ethics and the Limits of Philosophy, Morality, Shame and Necessity, *and* Truth and Truthfulness. *His influential critical discussion of utilitarianism appeared in* Utilitarianism: For and Against *(with J.J.C. Smart). Many of his essays have been collected in* Problems of the Self, Moral Luck, *and* Making Sense of Humanity. *This interview was conducted at Oxford in December 2002 by Alex Voorhoeve of The London School of Economics. Alex Voorhoeve's work was supported by the Analysis Trust Studentship 2003-2004. Unfortunately, Bernard Williams did not have the opportunity to correct the transcript of the interview.*

This shows in my philosophical work, on which Classical thought has had an important influence.

HRP: Which of your teachers and contemporaries most influenced you?

Williams: Though I did not agree with his views, I admired many of Gilbert Ryle's attitudes toward philosophy. I particularly learned from his criticism of dividing philosophy into what he called 'isms' and schools of philosophy. He believed there were many philosophical questions and ways of arguing about them, but that attaching labels like 'physicalism' or 'idealism' to any particular way of answering philosophical questions was extremely mechanical and also misleading. In general, I thought that Ryle was an extremely sensible, open-minded, and fair-minded teacher. I was also very impressed and influenced by my friend David Pears. In the fifties, when I was a young don, David and I gave classes together, and I very much admired his methods. Another person who had *one* kind of influence on me—though I'm glad to say I think she didn't influence me in other ways!—was Elizabeth Anscombe. One thing that she did, which she got from Wittgenstein, was that she impressed upon one that being clever wasn't enough. Oxford philosophy, and this is still true to a certain extent, had a great tendency to be clever. It was very eristic: there was a lot of competitive dialectical exchange and showing that other people were wrong. I was quite good at all that. But Elisabeth conveyed a strong sense of the seriousness of the subject, and how the subject was difficult in ways that simply being clever wasn't going to get around.

HRP: What is required in addition to being clever?

Williams: A good appreciation of what is *not* there in the argument or on the page, and also some imagination. Many philosophers pursue a line of argument in a very linear fashion, in which one proof caps another proof, or a refutation refutes some other supposed proof, instead of thinking laterally about what it all might mean. There is a tendency to forget the main issue, which is what the distinction that was made was supposed to be doing in the first place. An obvious example is that people used to go on about what the difference is between a moral and a non-moral 'this-that-and-the-other'. What is a moral consideration as opposed to a non-moral consideration? What is a moral judgement as opposed to a non-moral judgment? They belabored these questions without ever asking why the distinction was supposed to be so important in the first place.

HRP: What are your aims and motives in doing philosophy?

Williams: Stuart Hampshire used to say that historically, there have been two aims or motives for philosophy. One was curiosity and the other was salvation [laughs]. Plato, as he managed to combine almost everything else, combined the two [laughs again]. I think that Wittgenstein was very much on the side of salvation. So was Kierkegaard, though he was so clever that curiosity was always catching him out.

Now, I'm not into salvation. I suppose my interest in philosophy is primarily a curiosity that stems from puzzlement. It is the old philosophical motive of *simply not seeing* how various ideas which are supposed to be central to human life or human activities hang together. The notion of the self, obviously, the notion of moral and aesthetic value, and what place is taken by certain kinds of valuation, for example in works of art, in relation to life as a whole. Yes; some of it is in that sense just puzzlement.

But I suppose there are two other emphases in my work. First, granted my temperament, my curiosity was always aligned with suspiciousness. What Ricoeur has called the 'hermeneutic of suspicion', which was so characteristic in the 19th and 20th centuries in Nietzsche, Marx, and Freud, came rather naturally to me, with the result that the pretensions of certain kinds of value always aroused my suspicion.

The other development which has been more gradual in my work is that as a matter of fact, if you are puzzled by any idea that matters in human affairs, like politics or ethics, it is almost certain that you won't actually resolve your puzzlement just by philosophical analysis. You almost certainly need to know the history of the term you are dealing with. This historicist turn has become more prominent in my work in the last ten or fifteen years.

HRP: Can you say more about your view of the role of historical understanding in ethics and political philosophy?

Williams: History, which I take in a broad sense, is important in various ways. First, it may present us with a problem about our views. When we ask why we came to use some concepts rather than others that were prevalent at an earlier time, we typically come to see that this history is not vindicatory. That is, we might like to see our ideas, like liberal ideas of equality and equal rights, as having won an argument against earlier conceptions, like those of the *ancien régime*. History, however, shows that though these ideas 'won', they didn't win an argument—for the standards or aims of the argument practiced by the proponents of liberal ideas were not shared by the defenders of the *ancien régime.* This brings home to us the historical contingency of our ideas and outlook.

Now, this contingency need not be a problem for us, in the sense that it might not undermine our confidence in our outlook. For the idea that a vindicatory history—one that showed that our ideas were better by standards that could have been accepted by their historical opponents—is what is required looks like the idea that we should search for a system of ethical and political ideas which is best from a point of view that is as free as possible from contingent historical perspective. And I believe it is an illusion to think that is our task. But though it may not lead us to reject our outlook, the fact that there is no vindicatory history of it does matter, for example, in our attitude towards the outlooks of others.

Second, history can help us understand particular ways in which our ideas seem incoherent to us. For instance, I believe liberalism has problems with ideas of autonomy which can be traced to Enlightenment conceptions of the individual that do not make sense to us.

Third, the content of ethical and political ideas that are useful for us will be determined in part by an understanding of the necessities of our way of life. The question, "What is possible for us now?" is, I believe, really a relevant consideration in political and moral philosophy. This question demands empirical social understanding and insight. I would claim that you are not going to get such insight except by historical methods. That is, I don't believe that there is, for instance, a substantive enough, or interesting enough, sociology which could tell you what is possible for us.

HRP: Can you give an example of these ways in which history is important for a political concept?

Williams: Take liberty. I think that, like other political concepts, what we need is to construct a concept of liberty that is historically self-conscious and suitable for a modern society. I distinguish between "primitive freedom"—being unobstructed in doing what you want by some form of humanly imposed coercion—and liberty.[2] Since liberty is a political value, to determine which losses of primitive freedom can count as a loss of liberty, and especially when considering what counts as 'humanly imposed coercion', we have to consider what someone could reasonably resent as a loss. Here the question of the form of society that is possible for us becomes relevant. From this perspective, a practice is not a limitation of liberty if it is necessary for there to be any state at all. But it is also not a loss of liberty if it is necessary for the functioning of society as we can reasonably imagine it working and still being 'our' society. Thus, while some force and threats of force, and some institutional structures which impose disadvantage on people will count as limiting people's liberty, being prevented from getting what I want through economic competition will not, except in exceptional cases. That is because competition is central to modern, commercial society's functioning.

Understanding our historical condition also helps us understand the value that liberty has for us. The concept of modernity I have in mind here is the sense in which the concept of modernity is roughly the foundation of modern social science. It is roughly, Weber's concept of modernity, and related notions. That involves the disenchantment of the world and the retreat from believing that the order of how people should treat one another is somehow inscribed either in them or in the universal realm. It also involves an associated tendency to hold up various traditional sources of authority to question; it is a notable feature of modernity that we do not believe the traditional legitimation stories of hierarchy and inequality.

Now, the link between modernity and the value of liberty is as follows. It is because we start with less in telling our own legitimation stories than other outlooks that liberty is more important to us. Because of our doubts about authority, we allow each citizen a strong presumption in favor of carrying out his or her own desires.

This admittedly very rough account of liberty also illustrates how a historical explanation of the value a concept has for us need not undermine it. For we can regard our current mistrust of the legitimation stories of the past as a good thing, because it is a consequence of the fact that under the conditions of modernity we have a better grasp on the truth.

HRP: I'd like to turn to your view of what modernity, and the reflective consciousness it implies, means for our view of ethics. One part of the ethical you focus on is the virtues. I want to focus on the case of someone who doesn't possess these virtues, and who is thinking about acquiring them. As you discuss in *Ethics and the Limits of Philosophy*, Aristotle had an answer for such a person—even though the person might not be able to appreciate the answer or find it attractive from the perspective of his current plans and desires. [3] He believed that each kind of thing had an ideal form of functioning. This ideal form of functioning for human beings consisted of a state of happiness or, as you prefer to call it, well-being— a state which required the possession of the virtues. But we no longer believe Aristotle's assumptions about the natural striving of each kind of thing towards its perfection. So do *we* have an answer for this person?

Williams: Yes, good. I think this is like a lot of features of modernity. There is an increase in insight, in knowledge, in irony, and a decrease in all-around satisfaction about the world all fitting together. Actually I believe, although I don't think I've made this as clear as I could have in *Ethics and the Limits of Philosophy*, that Aristotle's own account, which from the *Nichomachean Ethics* emerges as a pretty satisfied account of the virtues, is an astonishing piece of cultural wish-fulfillment. Because that absolutely cannot have been what Athens in the 4th century BC was all about. If you consider the Athens of which Plato gave a far more honest and realistic, though also jaundiced, picture, and you consider that it was on its way after all to the collapse of democracy, then the idea that all these people were swimming around in this state of huge self-satisfaction and in harmony with the universe and the polity and their own desires is completely ridiculous. Aristotle was a provincial who became exceedingly impressed by a conservative view of a certain kind.

HRP: But in *Ethics and the Limits of Philosophy*, you present our disbelief of Aristotle's assumptions as undermining our ethical confidence. If they could scarcely be believed at the time the ancient views of the virtues were developed, then how important could this justification have been for the confidence with which the view was held? If acquiring the virtues is, as Aristotle thought, a matter of being brought up in a certain way, and not a matter of a conscious undertaking, and if we accept that these virtues *are* going to be attractive to us when we have some of the dispositions that they require, then what does the falling away of the external justification for them do to our view of the value of the virtues?

Williams: I think these are extremely good questions. I think you have to take what I was saying there in the context of a certain assumption which I had already identified which that discussion falls under. Rather early in the book, in the second chapter, I do question an issue, an assumption, which some moral philosophers make, which is that it is going to make a whole lot of difference what the answer to the question about external justification is going to be. I do say that it seems rather odd that it should be so, for I ask, "What is the professor's argument to do when they come to take him away?" But going with the assumption that the philosophical justification of the ethical is going to make some difference, this is the place at which it is going to make some difference. Now, in Aristotle's case, I don't think he delivers on his promise to show how they all hang together in an attractive package. But since I don't believe that the question about the philosophical justification of the objectivity of ethics has quite the foundational or all-changing role which that assumes, you are quite right in saying that this external perspective doesn't seem to make quite so much difference.

But I do think that there is a point to be made, as so often in moral philosophy, which consists of turning the same point round, in a way, 180 degrees. The trouble is that if you get a story which presents an idealized account of the ethical in the virtue repertoire by stressing the unity of the virtues and their unity with happiness and all that, what this encourages, or can encourage, is its dialectical opposite. When the news gets out that for the vast majority of human beings the virtues don't necessarily go together, that some of them are a great disadvantage—and actually this is not great news; that the virtues can do you some harm was extremely well-known to Socrates, for instance—there is a strong tendency to say, "The whole of the ethical is bogus." The business of defending some of the ethical becomes much harder. So we come to a point where most of my efforts have been concentrated: to make *some* sense of the ethical as opposed to throwing out the whole thing because you can't have the idealized version of it.

HRP: Throughout the book there is a theme that self-consciousness, intellectual criticism, and knowledge destroy both Greek and

Enlightenment ideals. Still, the Greek way of thinking about morality seems to emerge less damaged than modern ways of thinking...

Williams: You are right that up to a point there are quite a few Greek ideas that are more robust, that have more material to give us, than more recent ideas. Though that's true, it is only true with heavy qualifications. The reason is that they are less dependent on certain optimistic practices, they are less indebted to ideas of free will of an overambitious kind. I think that the more exposed parts of modern ideas, that are in worse shape, are the bits that have to do with Christianity. The one exception is Hume, but Hume is very consciously operating in a pagan perspective. The weakness of Greek thought of course is, as I say in *Shame and Necessity*, that a set of ideas that arose from a totally different period, over 2000 years ago, will be totally out of place in the modern world.[4] There are some conceptions, particularly of rights, which have emerged, which we simply can't do without. The idea that we could would be ridiculous. Once we realize this, we must try to get these ideas which we can't do without into a shape where they need less metaphysical fuel than they do in the form given to them by Kant.

HRP: One current set of ideas that self-consciously is less dependent on metaphysics is contractualism, as expounded by Scanlon for example.[5] This doesn't seem to be susceptible to the same criticisms you level at other Enlightenment ideas. Scanlon even jokingly characterized his account of morality as offering "Kant on the cheap."[6]

Williams: [laughs] I think he's selling himself short!

HRP: Scanlon has an interesting idea about characterizing moral motivation as originating in the desire to be able to justify ourselves to others. As he puts it, the reason to act morally is the reason we have to not place ourselves in a position of revealed or concealed antagonism to others. What struck me is when you discuss the virtue of Sincerity in *Truth and Truthfulness*, you place a lot of emphasis on the kinds of relationships with others this virtue makes possible. You give an example of an old woman to whom we lie for her own benefit, and you say that though much of what Kant says about lying is mistaken, what is right about the Kantian account is that it focuses on how our relationship to her changes when we lie to her. As you write: "It is a violation of trust. I lead the hearer to rely on what I say, when she has good reason to do so, and in abusing this I abuse the relationship which is based on it. Even if it is for good reasons of concern for her, I do not give her a chance, in this particular respect, to form her own reactions to the facts.... Replacing the world in its impact on her by [a picture of it which is the product of] my will, I put her, to that extent, in my power and so take away or limit her freedom."[7] And that human beings have reasons for developing and maintaining relationships of trust forms part of the

solution to your question where the intrinsic (as opposed to instrumental) value of this disposition lies.

Williams: It is, as they say, no accident, comrade, that in *Truth and Truthfulness* I write in the chapter about lying, that I am very much in agreement with, and indebted to, Scanlon's book.[8] I also think that Scanlon's book has been misunderstood and unfairly treated. You will remember the criterion, which is about rules which others can't reasonably reject. It has been complained that there is no criterion for what they can't reasonably reject. But of course I take it that the point is just that *that* is the question we should be asking, and what goes into 'reasonable rejection' is just what we should be thinking about.

So I am quite sympathetic to this formulation. Certainly, it both doesn't require all the metaphysical baggage, that's true, and it also has the right shape to be a formula for a moral consideration, since equality of some kind is a core moral idea. It has to be understood that we have to understand the precondition of the Kingdom of Ends, that is, the set of persons whose conditions are regulated by the contractual test, on the basis of equality. Because you see, if you collectively think of the other outlooks as being the outlooks of the *ancien régime*, or indeed of the Greeks, then the idea that the core of morality has to do with what *anybody* could not reasonably reject is simply a non-starter. The fact that our acts and institutions could reasonably be rejected by some classes of persons is either not an issue or entirely foreseeable. No doubt the lower order wouldn't want to accept some principles by which the higher orders live, but from the perspective of the higher orders, that's of no consequence: they are lower, and so don't count as much. Of course the trouble then is how far that notion of equality, which is itself a moral notion, is constitutive, or as it were, 'factual', and how far is it an aspiration that is itself expressed by this way of treating people.

HRP: What would it be for it to be "factual"?

Williams: Well, I think that does have a bite. For I think that when you get people to reflect on the bases of discrimination, you then do get into the area of the factual. One way of putting it is this. In the past, people have discriminated against other people, not treated them equally in a Scanlonian or Kantian sense, because they were people of color or because they were women. Yet, it is not that "because she is a woman" or "because he is black" was really much of a reason. Roughly, it wasn't articulated in this way at all, it was just an inherent practice. When someone raises the question why they are so discriminated against, they have to start with a different kind of justification, such as "blacks are stupid," or "women don't have the requisite skills and character for certain jobs." But these were just rationalizations, false consciousnesses really, to support the institutions in question. Now, it is very important that these claims are false and known, in a sense, to be false. Take the case of the slave-owners who drafted the *Bill of Rights*. There was a great deal of false consciousness there, since when these slave owners took advantage of their women slaves, they didn't actually think they were engaged in bestiality.

HRP: I would have expected you to be more critical of contractualism...

Williams: Well, I think that it does raise a whole class of problems about one's relations to other people. Though it is probably not a criticism to raise these problems, since they are probably problems anyway. Contractualism is likely to give rise to what I call the 'one thought too many problem'.[9] Because no doubt one could make it a rule that other people could not reasonably reject that people should save their own spouses from the wreck, but it is not *that* thought that, one would hope, motivates the person who saves his spouse from a shipwreck. So there is always the question about the relationship between moral considerations and considerations of a non-reflective, or non-morally mediated, kind. But then I think you could say that that problem exists anyway.

HRP: But you could say something more in this situation. There are two different questions here. The first is "how are people acting in such a situation, what's going through their heads?", and the second is the reflective question about our habits of acting. The reflective question seems to me to be perfectly sensible, since we can't always follow the demands of friendship or love, and we need some perspective from which we evaluate how far it is morally permissible to act from these motives.

Williams: Well, up to a point. What you say is perfectly sensible, but if you go too far in that direction you get into the false disjunction between justification and motivation which Sidgwick and other, higher-order utilitarians make an enormous amount of, namely that so-and-so is the justification of acting in a certain way doesn't mean that it should enter into the motivations of the people who are so acting. I think that leads to an absurd alienation problem. I mean, up to a point there is a possibility there, but in the end one needs a unity between the language and thought of action and the language and thought of reflection.

HRP: In *Moral Luck* you remark that an idea of ethical consistency that demanded that an action being morally justified implies that no one can justifiably complain from the moral point of view is too strong, and you give the example of political cases, where one can be justified in an action that comes at a moral cost of harming others.[10]

Williams: In the political case, I indeed think you cannot say of the people who have to bear the burden of the decision that they have no justified complaint, that they haven't been wronged since they should take the perspective of the *raison d'état*.

HRP: What about the individual case, where someone might do what is morally right, but still wrong someone in the process? Do you think this conflicts with Scanlon's contractualism, which doesn't seem to allow for such conflicts?

Williams: I was sort of glancing at that when I made the earlier point. The difficulty is the usual level of description problem. Nobody could reasonably reject, in the Scanlonian sense, there being such an institution as promising. And moreover, they can't reasonably reject the idea that there are certain kinds of circumstances in which it is justified to break those promises. Now, there will then be a set of issues about how far down you would go with principles that you apply the question to. For instance, if I have broken a promise, does that mean I should recompense or apologize to the parties I have disadvantaged? Well if so, if there is an 'ought' there, as there seems to be, then that seems to imply that nobody could reasonably reject a rule that requires that I give compensation, or an apology, *et cetera*. But I must say that I think we are clearer there that recompense is appropriate than about the fact that it is a principle that no one could reasonably reject that one should offer recompense in such situations. We are reading back from the intuition into the formula. Now, does it mean that the recipient of the apology ought to accept it? That is very unclear. Or does it mean that the recipient of the apology either ought to accept it or ought to disagree that the principle on which I was acting was not reasonably rejectable by him?

HRP: I think it does have this implication.

Williams: Well, it looks to me that when you get too far down here, you get the idea that everybody's responses would be harmonized in a way that would suit the Kingdom of Ends (which would be better named the Republic of Ends, if you ask me!). So we come to the usual problem with contractualism, that it requires too much harmonization of people's moral sentiments. We all know of situations in which people would, perfectly intelligibly, refuse to play this game of giving reasons for and against general principles.

HRP: I'd like to turn to your work on truth and modern culture. Nietzsche wrote that "man is a venerating animal, but also a mistrustful one; and that the world is *not* worth what we thought is about the most certain thing our mistrust has finally gotten hold of." He also wrote: "The more mistrust, the more philosophy."[11] Do you think mistrust (rather than veneration) is characteristic of modern society—and does it make for "more philosophy"?

Williams: Yes. But there is a heavy qualification coming. That is that the effect of modern entertainment, modern communication, modern saturation with 'information', may make effective criticism, or effective reflection impossible. Just as the tabloid newspapers get obsessed with the day's scandal, and the Internet becomes dominated by the same kind of 'news', it is possible that this so-called self-searching and questioning becomes just another superficial phenomenon, and that there are simply a lot of unquestioned assumptions about how life is being led that are really quite unsatisfactory. If expressed, I don't think people would really believe in them, but they have no option but to go along with them. I think that if one means *effective* criticism and self-searching, there is a very big question-mark over it. Of course a lot of what one has in mind when one thinks about social critics, I mean conservative social critics on the one hand and defenders of liberalism on the other, is a very intense and serious form of criticism which was the product of modernity, when the thinker was still protected by the institutions of an earlier time. Now these institutions themselves have devolved into one gigantic market, it is very unclear whether anyone will have thoughts of this highly directed kind at all. So the idea of a space in which philosophy and related kinds of critical and questioning activity can go on may itself be under threat.

HRP: In *Truth and Truthfulness*, you also suggest that our culture of suspicion threatens to undermine our faith in truth. You begin with Nietzsche's discussion of the ideal of truthfulness. Nietzsche comes to the conclusion that truthfulness is the last metaphysical concept, and that the investigation that is driven by truthfulness ends up undermining itself.

Williams: In *The Gay Science* and *The Genealogy of Morality,* when Nietzsche says that this fire that burns in our inquiries is that self-same fire that burns in Plato,[12] he intends to upset the liberals who have been very happily nodding along with him while he is being rude to the church. He certainly wanted, I think, an account of the value of truthfulness which would be adequately naturalized. I hope the book to some extent offers that by constructing a genealogy of truth. A genealogy is a narrative that tries to explain an outlook or value by describing how it came about, or could have come about, or could be imagined to come about. An interesting question one can ask of such genealogies is whether they are vindicatory, that is, whether the genealogical account of a value, when it is understood, strengthens or weakens one's confidence in that value. A vindicatory genealogy makes sense of a particular value, although it doesn't quite make sense of it in the elevated terms in which others have described it. The basis then doesn't have to be metaphysical.

The further question is of course whether our commitment to truthfulness leads to tragedy or to everybody being happier. Nietzsche was occupied with this question, and in my view rightly so. My book is optimistic about the possibility of naturalizing truthfulness, but I leave you to judge the last pages to find out whether I am optimistic or pessimistic [about this further question]. Several people have said they can't make out whether the end of my book is optimistic or pessimistic, and I think that is right.

HRP: I thought your book ended with a pious hope about truth and truthfulness...

Williams: It certainly isn't a *pious* hope! The last writer I quote is Conrad in *Heart of Darkness*.[13] As they say in New York: "think about it." φ

Notes:

[1] Baggini, J., "Beating the Systems," *The Philosophers' Magazine,* no. 21 (2003): 29.
[2] Williams, Bernard. "From Freedom to Liberty: The Construction of a Political Value," *Philosophy & Public Affairs,* no.30 (2001): 3-26.
[3] Williams, Bernard, *Ethics and the Limits of Philosophy* (Cambridge: Harvard University Press, 1985), ch. 3.
[4] Williams, Bernard, *Shame and Necessity* (Berkeley: University of California Press, 1993).
[5] Scanlon, T.M., *What We Owe to Each Other* (Cambridge: Harvard University Press, 1998). Also, Scanlon, T.M., "Metaphysics and Morals," *Proceedings and Addresses of the American Philosophical Association (2002-2003):* 7-22.
[6] Voorhoeve, A., "Kant on the Cheap," *The Philosophers' Magazine,* no.16 (2001): 29-30.
[7] Williams, Bernard, *Truth and Truthfulness* (Cambridge: Harvard University Press, 2002), 118.
[8] Ibid. ch. 5.
[9] Williams, Bernard, "Persons, Character, and Morality," in *Moral Luck* (Cambridge: Cambridge University Press, 1981), 1-19.
[10] Williams, Bernard, "Moral Luck" and "Politics and Moral Character," in *Moral Luck* (Cambridge: Cambridge University Press, 1981), 20-39 and 54-70.
[11] Nietzsche, Friedrich, *The Gay Science,* ed. Bernard Williams, trans. J. Nauckhoff (Cambridge: Cambridge University Press, 2000), sec. 346, p. 204.
[12] "But you will have gathered what I'm getting at, namely, that it is still a *metaphysical faith* upon which our faith in science rests—that even we knowers of today, we godless anti-metaphysicians, still take *our* fire, too, from the flame lit by thousand-year-old faith, the Christian faith which was also Plato's faith, that God is truth; that truth is divine..." Nietzsche, Friedrich, *The Gay Science,* ed. Bernard Williams, trans. J. Nauckhoff (Cambridge: Cambridge University Press, 2000), sec. 344, p. 201.
[13] The quoted passage is one where the narrator in *Heart of Darkness* says about Kurtz and his dying words:

> This is the reason why I affirm that Kurtz was a remarkable man. He had something to say. He said it ...he had summed up—he had judged. 'The horror!' He was a remarkable man. After all, this was the expression of some sort of belief; it had candour, it had conviction, it had a vibrating note of revolt in its whisper; it had the appalling face of a glimpsed truth....

Conrad, Joseph, *Youth. Heart of Darkness. The End of the Tether* (London: J.M. Dent and Sons, 1946), 151.

Toward a Unified Theory of Reality

An Interview with John Searle

HRP: I want to start by asking how you got interested in philosophy. Did you always know you were going to be doing this?

Searle: Well I didn't always know I would be a professional philosopher. But there is a sense in which I have always been interested in philosophical problems. Even when I was a very small child I was interested in philosophical problems....

HRP: Which ones?

Searle: Things like: Does God exist? Do we really have free will? Things like that—the kind of thing that occurs to any bright child, brought up in our civilization. I think thoughtful children are bound to worry about things like that. Now, I did not worry about 'referential opacity', or the 'Open Question Argument'—that came later. But, I have always been interested in philosophical problems. And I hung out with a bunch of intellectually self-conscious people in high school—that is, they were self-conscious about being intellectual—and we used to discuss philosophical issues all the time. We read Nietzsche and Schopenhauer and other such people, and I read Russell's *History of Western Philosophy* when I was still a teenager. So I have always been interested in the subject, but it was not really until I got to Oxford that I began seriously

John R. Searle is Mills Professor of the Philosophy of Mind and Language at the University of California at Berkeley. His many books include: Speech Acts, Expression and Meaning, Intentionality, The Mystery of Consciousness, *and* Consciousness and Language. *He has taught popular undergraduate courses and graduate seminars regularly at UC Berkeley for the past forty years, and his books have been translated into over twenty languages. This interview was conducted by Zoë Sachs-Arellano in August 2003 in Berkeley.*

considering a professional career in it. I was only 19 when I first arrived in Oxford, and I matriculated not long after my twentieth birthday. At that time, philosophy was the most exciting subject taught in Oxford. It was a great time to be alive as a student of philosophy, and I was very much excited by the philosophical activity going on, and gradually it became clear to me that this is really what I wanted to do as a profession. So you might say there are two questions. One is: When did you get into it professionally? And the answer to that is in Oxford. And the other one is: How long have you been interested in philosophy? And the answer is always.

HRP: What were the main areas that really got you at first? Did it change over time?

Searle: It did. When I was in Oxford, *the* most exciting field *by far* was the philosophy of language. And the most exciting people in it were two of my teachers—J. L. Austin and Peter Strawson. So my first interest was the philosophy of language, and my first two books in philosophy were on the philosophy of language. But in an interesting kind of way, those opened up several other areas of philosophy to me. I was lucky that I picked for my first major research project something that was so open-ended, because it led out in one direction into the mind, and in another direction into society. So, though my interests in the subject have expanded, they have not in any sense made a U-turn. That is, they have just expanded what was already implicit in the theory of speech acts.

HRP: Can you point to your first big breakthrough, maybe in the philosophy of language?

Searle: Yes. That has often happened to me, that I have had breakthroughs. One of my breakthroughs was when I was trying to state the conditions for the successful performance of a speech act of a certain kind, such as promising. I suddenly saw it. I had not seen it when I was a student and a faculty member in Oxford. I was already teaching at Berkeley when I got this. I had my first breakthrough when I saw how to construct the necessary and sufficient conditions for what I call a successful and non-defective performance of a speech act. Then I had other breakthroughs along the way, such as when I suddenly saw that the whole orthodox view about what then was called the naturalistic fallacy was in a sense self-contradictory because the version that was put to us was: you cannot derive an evaluative statement from a descriptive statement—no such entailment can ever be valid. But the problem is that notions like "derivation" and "validity" are already evaluative notions, so the paradox was that the standard way of stating the impossibility of something—namely, getting logical relations between what was normative and what was factual—presupposed *precisely* that you could state such logical relations.

HRP: In a past interview you said that one of the key things to being a good philosopher is openness.

Searle: Yes....

HRP: ...willingness to actually challenge your most fundamental views.

Searle: Absolutely, yes.

HRP: Has that happened to you in the past? That you had to do that?

Searle: Well there is a sense in which I didn't have to work very hard at it, because everyone seems to be always challenging my views. I have benefited from the fact that a lot of my work has been the subject of conferences and debates and attacks in the philosophy journals, as well as volumes of critical articles—there was one called *John Searle and His Critics*, and there is another one that has just come out edited by Barry Smith, called *John Searle*—so I benefited a lot from the kind of criticism I got. Now I have to confess that I have a flaw: my *natural* impulse is to *defend* myself like a tiger when attacked. And I think that is a natural impulse you have in philosophy; but as I get older, I try to restrain that impulse and ask myself not, What kind of mistakes is this attacker making? But, What can I learn from these attacks? So I do try to learn from criticism, absolutely. I mean there are some issues where I have been attacked a lot where I really don't have any worries—I guess the most famous is the 'Chinese Room Argument'. People are still attacking me on that, but [chuckles], it's *so* simple, I really don't have any worries about that argument. But there are other things, like my theory of 'Intentionality', or the analysis of speech acts, or my conception of rationality, and I learn a lot from arguments about those.

HRP: In the case of the Chinese Room Argument, the reason why you are convinced of it is a deeper reason than what was in the original argument.

Searle: I have always found the original argument convincing as it stands. The argument expresses something that I think is fairly obvious—I think it is kind of a tautology. Namely, you have to make a distinction between syntax and semantics, and syntax is not the same as nor is it sufficient for semantics. So, the syntax of the implemented program—the zeroes and ones, or the Chinese symbols, or whatever—is not sufficient to constitute, nor is it sufficient to guarantee the presence of, semantic content. The argument is so simple—it doesn't take higher-level mathematics to see the point.

HRP: Right, and then even *syntax* you think is actually....

Searle: Well now that is a deeper point: the syntax itself is not intrinsic to the physics of the system, because syntax is observer-relative. It took me a *long* time to see that. In the old Chinese Room days I *gave* them the zeroes and the ones—they can have the syntax. I also gave them the Turing test—just assume the system passes the Turing Test. What I showed—what I tried to show—is that the fact that an implemented program consisting entirely of syntactical manipulations can pass the Turing test does not have the implications they think it does. Because you can have all the syntax you want, you can pass the Turing Test, and still not understand anything. But then later on it dawned on me that I was conceding too much to give them the zeroes and the ones, because zeroes and ones are not part of natural science. They are not observer-independent features of reality, they exist relative to our interpretation.

HRP: So we have to actually count the....

Searle: We have to decide what we are going to count as a *symbol*. Nature knows nothing of symbols. We have to impose symbolism on nature.

HRP: I get the feeling that philosophy is more than just what you do for a living.

Searle: Oh absolutely, I *love* it. I *love* it.

HRP: Do you do it a lot when you're at home?

Searle: Oh yes. My wife was trained as a professional philosopher so we talk philosophy frequently. She has a graduate degree from Oxford and then eventually became a lawyer, in part because in those days, you couldn't get a job in the same university as your spouse—there were anti-nepotism rules. Also when my kids were really young we used to have a game we played at the dinner table called Semantic Analysis. And kids are natural philosophers—you ask the kids, "How do you know you're not now dreaming?" and they will come up with very surprising answers. So you ask them *traditional* philosophical questions, and sometimes it's hard to make the question clear, but in general kids come up with exciting ideas. So I do philosophy all the time. I dream philosophy, and I tend to interpret non-philosophical things that I'm reading in a philosophical way.

NATURE AND REALISM

HRP: Just now you said that we "impose symbolism on nature." What exactly do you mean when you talk about "nature," or observer-independent reality? What counts as part of nature for you?

Searle: What we are talking about here is that part of the world that is observer-independent. Of course everything is part of nature, including us and our culture and all the rest of it, but what I mean is that there is a fundamental distinction, that philosophers tend to lose sight of, between those features of the world that exist regardless of us—which, so to speak, don't give a damn about us—and those that depend on us for their existence, or at least for their existence under a certain description. So, the fact that there is a certain piece of paper that has certain marks on it—that fact is observer-independent, that is, so to speak, part of nature. But the fact that that piece of paper is a dollar bill—that fact is relative to us, that is observer-relative or observer-dependent. Now the fundamental question here is: What about computation? Is it observer-relative or observer-independent? Of course there are computations that are completely observer-independent, that go on regardless of what anybody thinks. If I now think to myself "2+2=4," that is intrinsically a computation. And if somebody says, "Well, we don't interpret you as computing," too bad for them. Regardless of what observers think, I am computing, I am doing arithmetic! But when I have a pocket calculator and it shows: 2+2=4, that computation exists only relative to our interpretation because the actual pocket calculator knows nothing about computing—it is just an electrical machine, just a hunk of junk, just a certain electronic circuit with a set of state transitions, and up on its little screen comes the numeral "4." But the calculator doesn't know that it is doing addition, or that 4 is a number, or that these are numerals, because it does not know anything. Now that's the distinction I'm getting at: between actually thinking something to yourself where there is some conscious thought process going on—that is observer-independent; and those features that exist relative to us, relative to our interpretation. And the point I make is, you don't discover computation in nature—you can't discover syntax in nature, you assign it to processes. *Computation is not discovered, it's assigned*, with the exception of computations that you actually do in a conscious mind.

HRP: Okay, so you do think we can talk about an uninterpreted, meaningless, view-from-nowhere reality that's out there.

Searle: Sure we can. And it is there, absolutely. I'm the most naïve of naïve realists: there is a real world that exists completely independent of us, that doesn't give a damn about us.

HRP: What about the entities in scientific theories—are those observer-relative?

Searle: Here is my view exactly. It is a matter of historical accident that I have to have professional help to find out that hydrogen atoms have one electron, but I do not have to have professional help to find out that I have one nose. But the ontological status of my one nose and that of the one electron are exactly the same. They are real parts of the real world.

Electrons function causally; you can actually, so to speak, "see" them in cloud chambers and bubble chambers. I think this whole dispute about the existence of theoretical entities is a residue of verificationism and positivism. But I think of course if electrons really exist then they really exist. In this respect, they are just like noses and thumbs. It is just an accident of our history that we can't see an electron and we can see a nose. We have to have professional help to find out how many electrons there are, but we don't need professional help to find out how many noses there are. That is my attitude towards these theoretical entities. If they really exist, they really exist.

HRP: Well how about the case of our normal observation without professional help—do you think there's no interpretation built in to that?

Searle: For me, as you know, all perception has interpretation built into it. Interpretation is made possible by what I call the 'background.' The background consists of our presupposed capacities for coping with the world. You cannot perceive without a set of background capacities. My dog, just as a pure matter of his visual apparatus, has a much better visual mechanism than I do, but I see all kinds of things that he can't see because I have a richer set of background capacities—I can see things like words and letters, and people looking unhappy, and advertisements for cars, and all sorts of things that are a function of my interpretation. And even for the dog, in order that he can interpret an event as perceiving me, or as perceiving something to eat—requires a background. So for me there is no such thing as "unadulterated" or "pure" perception. To put it in my jargon, the perception only determines its conditions of satisfaction *relative* to a set of background capacities, that are not a part of the perceptual experience, but that are the conditions of the possibility of the perceptual experience having the content that it does.

HRP: Right, so I guess my question is: Why do you say that what we observe is observer-independent?

Searle: Because it's there, regardless of whether or not we observe it. You have to have a perceptual and cognitive apparatus to see two thumbs, but the two thumbs are there. Similarly, you have to have an apparatus in order to see that there's a tree out there. The confusion of the epistemic conditions for knowing with the ontology of what is known is one of the oldest mistakes in philosophy. There are a number of famous disasters that derive from supposing that because perception is always mediated— for example, it is always from a point of view and under certain categories—we cannot perceive the real world. Kant's transcendental idealism is one of the most famous disasters. He tried to derive idealism— or his peculiar form of transcendental idealism—from the fact that perception is always mediated by the categories and by our perceptual apparatus. But it doesn't follow from the fact that the perception is mediated that you do not actually perceive the real world.

HRP: Yet it seems like it would almost be a matter of faith whether or not you want to believe that we're actually perceiving the world as it is independently of us.

Searle: There are two separate issues: Is there a real world that exists independently of our representations? And that I want to say is not a thesis that you can argue for. It is a presupposition of having theses; it is a background presupposition, and I try to spell that out—I think it's in the end of *The Construction of Social Reality* that I talk about metaphysical realism or external realism as a presupposition of all kinds of use of language. I don't think there is an intermediate position between solipsism and realism; I don't think you can adopt an intermediate position. Because if you allow that you and I communicate, then you have to presuppose that there is a common reality that we can communicate *about*. And if you allow that I can ask such questions as "Shall I go to Chicago next week?" then you have to allow that I am presupposing the existence of an independent reality. So there are several different questions we don't want to confuse: One is external realism, or metaphysical realism—I don't care what we call it, but it is the idea that there is a reality that exists independently of our perceptions of it. And I think it is a mistake to treat that as if it were a hypothesis, as if it were a theory. You have to treat it as a presupposition for having theories—it is part of the background. Now given that, then there is a separate question that arises: What is the relationship between our perceptual experience and this independently existing reality? And there I want to say I adhere to a kind of view of direct realism: in a favorable case you actually see objects, you see real objects, and you see them the way they are. However, that takes a great deal of apparatus—that is not simple, it is not a matter of just a straight impact of two objects, you have to have intentional causation and it has to be mediated by various neuro-biological and psychological capacities in your brain.

So just to summarize, we need to distinguish two positions. External realism says there is a way things are that exists independently of how we represent how they are. But within external realism, there are several possible positions. Within external realism we can have a view that perceptions give us knowledge of actual facts in the world.

THE MAIN QUESTION OF PHILOSOPHY

HRP: We should come back to both those points: that there is an independent reality, and that we directly observe it. But first, let me ask you a more general question. You said at one point that we (philosophers) have to start at a dumb stage, and just let ourselves be impressed by questions that may seem kind of dumb.

Searle: Yes, that's right.

HRP: But if they seem dumb maybe they don't naturally interest you, because you have to *make* yourself interested in them. What are the questions that *really* are the most fundamental, interesting questions to you, right now for example? I think it's probably something to do with consciousness—what problem keeps you up at night that you really want to solve?

Searle: First of all, you do not have to make yourself interested in these questions, rather you have to *recover* your pre-adult innocence. You have to become like a child again and regard as amazing facts that adults tend to take for granted.

There are a whole lot of problems like that that preoccupy me. For me the problem of consciousness has now gone from being a philosophical problem to being a neuro-biological problem. That is, I now think that what philosophers can do is get the problem in a shape where it admits of scientific treatment—and that is what I have tried to do with the subject of consciousness. I think there is now enough good research going on in neurobiology that it is not out of the question that we will have some real results in this field. The problem I am working on *right now*, the one that is really keeping me awake now, is how to extend the account of social reality and institutional reality that I gave in a book—*The Construction of Social Reality*—to a more general account of civilization. So I am working now on what I call—this is kind of a pretentious title, but anyway—the 'ontology of civilization'. And I think if I could just see how to tie the account of rationality that I gave in a book—*Rationality in Action*—with the account of social reality, I could get another breakthrough that would give me a more general account of civilization, a more general account of the ontology of human social reality, than I have so far.

HRP: So what's the top problem for contemporary philosophy to work on right now?

Searle: For my money, there's *exactly one problem*. And I have been working on it *all* my life, and there is a sense in which I didn't really *know* that that was the problem that I was working on until I had been working on it for ten years. The problem is this: We now know a lot about how the world works—to put it very crudely, we know the universe is made of physical particles in fields of force, these are characteristically organized into systems, and some of these systems are organic systems that have evolved over billions of years. Basically atomic theory and evolutionary biology are *absolutely foundational* for us. I *start* philosophy assuming them—they are not something I have to give a foundation to. Let us assume that's right—that the world is made of physical particles and we are the result of evolution. *Then the fundamental philosophical problem is how do we give an account of the human reality which is consistent with what we know from physics and chemistry?* That is, in a world consisting of meaningless physical particles, we take ourselves to be conscious, speech-act performing, intentional, social, political, free, rational beings. Now how can we make those conceptions of ourselves consistent with what we know about the world of brute facts? And in a sense that is what I have always been writing about—*Speech Acts* was about how we get from sound to meaning. And *Intentionality* is about how the mind has the capacity to represent, and so on with my other books. To me the number one question in philosophy is: How do you give a coherent account of the one, single universe, which will reconcile the human reality with the more basic reality, of which the human reality is only a small part? And maybe in some areas you can't make the two consistent, maybe we are going to have to give up on some of our self conceptions, such as, for example, free will. But my aim is to try to give a *coherent* systematic account. So I reject any kind of dualism, or any kind of tripartite distinction of the kind given by Popper, and even Frege.

Am I being clear—do you see what I'm saying?

HRP: Yes. You say you start with the "basic reality" of nature. How do you justify starting there, if we only experience that reality through our perceptions, through *our* human reality?

Searle: Epistemically, the human reality is primary, because you can't have knowledge of the real world without having consciousness and a reasoning capacity and so on. But if there is *one* overwhelming mistake in the past four hundred years of Western philosophy, it is the confusion of epistemology with ontology. Epistemology for me is *not* the fundamental branch of philosophy—it's a secondary branch. Ontology and the philosophy of language for me are *prior* to epistemology. So I agree that you have to have an epistemic basis for finding out about the real world, but once you find out about the real world, once you find out what it is made of and the basic principles of its operation, then those results are no longer epistemic results, they are results about what you know, not how you know it. These are basic results that you can then build on. So there is a sense in which I don't take traditional skepticism seriously. I think it was a disaster that we took it so seriously for so long. People thought, "Well, before we can ever do anything in philosophy, we have to solve the problem of induction and we have to prove the existence of the external world" and so on. I don't think that. I think that one of the good things that has happened in my lifetime is that epistemology has stopped being the central area of philosophy.

HRP: But how do you get over skepticism without just ignoring it and saying it doesn't matter?

Searle: Well okay—there are important things to be said about skepticism. Now when I say that skepticism is not central to philosophy, I don't mean that there isn't an interesting branch of philosophical investigation which has to do with dealing with skepticism. I have not devoted a great deal of my effort to that, but I can tell you that one of the things I discovered is that one of the ways that skepticism *gets going* is by treating elements of the background as if they were *theories* that had to be justified. So I think the DNA theory of genetics is a *theory*, but the idea that there is a real world that exists independently of us, that is not a theory. That is a presupposition, that is a *background* pre-condition for *having* theories. This is why we are always so embarrassed by efforts to prove "the existence of the external world." Kant said it's a scandal that no one has proven the existence of the external world. And, G. E. Moore said *I'll* prove the existence of the external world—here are two hands! But I want to say that they are both missing the point. Kant was wrong in thinking that we hold a theory that needs to be proven to the effect that there exists a reality to which our representations are answerable— that is not itself a theory. So Kant was wrong about that, and Moore just missed the point, if he thought Kant could be answered by holding up his hands.

HRP: So you don't think it can be true or false at all?

Searle: Anything that can be stated in a propositional form can be characterized as true or false. But you miss the point if you think that that implies that all background presuppositions are theories. Of course you can take any element of the background and hold it up for examination, but in normal discourse I say to you, "What are you going to do this afternoon? Did you keep your medical appointment? How is your car running? Do you like your new apartment?" The *intelligibility* of all of those *presupposes* that there is something we are talking about, that there are public objects of reference that exist independently of us. So it isn't that I have got a new proof of the external world—that's not it at all. Rather I want to say that *the presupposition* that *there is a way that things are,* is not itself another theory about how things are.

HRP: One problem that strikes me here is that, normally, we think of presuppositions as dogmas to be woken up from—as assumptions we ought to make explicit and critically evaluate. Is that different from your view of presuppositions?

Searle: Well, here is the trouble. The debates about this tend to have kind of a fruitless quality, because the presupposition of having the debate is that there is something that we can debate *about.* And so I want to say it is a mistake to suppose we can or should prove that presupposition.... I want to say that Kant was wrong because he thought that there could be a proof, and Moore was wrong to think that he had given a proof. I want to say, you have to ask yourself what makes proof possible, what are the conditions of possibility of *anything* being a proof or an argument or a statement. In a way, Wittgenstein is struggling with this same question in *On Certainty*. And we have had this illusion since I guess Descartes, but maybe since the Greeks, that somehow or other everything can be put up for grabs—that you can start philosophy from absolute ground zero and build a world from the inside out. If there is one thing that we know from the past three or four centuries, it is that it doesn't work, we can't do that.

Of course I haven't refuted total solipsism. I have not refuted the view that what I think of as the universe is my massive hallucination. But what I'm saying is, if I assume that you and I are actually communicating with each other, then I have already presupposed the shared world. We presuppose public objects of reference if we presuppose a public language. A public language requires a public world. That is the point.

HRP: So there *is* a certain amount of faith, in a certain sense.

Searle: Not exactly. The precondition of having any faith at all can't be just another item of faith.

HRP: You use the word "ontology" a lot, and many analytic philosophers tend to shy away from that word, because they say they don't know what it means, or that it is used in many different ways....

Searle: Well they use a word that I hate even more: "metaphysics."

HRP: How do those two relate?

Searle: I think I use 'ontology' because I am embarrassed to use the word 'metaphysics.' I was brought up to *throw up* whenever I heard the word 'metaphysics'—it just seemed like some weird branch of philosophy that had long since been discredited. But, by "ontology," I just mean that which has to do with existence. The question of what exists, and what the mode of its existence is—that's ontology. And I want to say that it's a mistake that we have made for centuries to suppose that the answer to *that* question has to be given epistemologically—that the mode of existence has to do with how you know about it. The verification principle was the leading statement of this confusion of epistemology with ontology, that the meaning of any sentence is given by how you would verify it. And I want to say: No, if the sentence in question is about how things really are, then you have to distinguish how we find out about something, and what it is that we find out about. So ontology isn't a tough notion for me, it just means what exists, and how it exists. But I think that's the way a lot of philosophers use the word "metaphysics."

HRP: Just to be sure: "exists" for you is some serious fact about the universe, and not just a property of the theories we're working with?

Searle: By "exists" I just mean exists. When I say something exists, I mean it's really there. "Exists" is a formal term and Frege taught us how it works: That is, when you say "horses exist," you are saying that the predicate "x is a horse" has instances. Something actually satisfies the predicate. When we say horses exist, we are talking about the real world and not about language or theories. I am not one of these people who thinks "things only exist relative to a theory"—I can't make any sense out of that. Because I want to know: Is the theory true?

HRP: Okay, and "true"?

Searle: "True" means—with qualifications that I give—correspondence to reality. Now there are famous difficulties with some versions of the correspondence theory of truth but I think if it is carefully stated and appropriately understood, none of these difficulties are serious. I try to show how, properly understood, disquotation implies the correspondence conception of truth.

REALISM AND TRUTH

HRP: Let's go to your view of *direct* realism, and your reasons for thinking that what exists to our eyes is the same as what exists, period. The access to the observer-independent ontology doesn't worry you at all?

Searle: I don't give any special status to "our eyes." They are products of our evolutionary history. But when we discover something using "our eyes" then typically what we discover exists independently of its discovery. You see, methodological questions, questions about how to find out about the world, it seems to me, always have the same answer. Where methodology is concerned, use any weapon you can lay your hands on, and stay with any weapon that works. If you use cloud chambers for finding out about particles and they seem to work pretty well, you stick with that. And if somebody invents a bubble chamber and now you have a better method for finding out about the movement of particles—you go with the best method. But there isn't any simple algorithmic answer for what is the right method for finding out about the truth.

HRP: Right. But why do you assume that *any* of the methods we use give us access to the observer-independent reality? Why must direct realism *necessarily* be the case, instead of Kant's phenomena or something like that?

Searle: Direct realism isn't "necessarily" the case, but it so happens that evolution has given us sensory modalities, especially sight and touch, by way of which we can often get direct perceptual access to objects and states of affairs in the world.

We have actually found out a lot of things. For me the problem with skepticism is this: the single most stunning intellectual fact about the past two or three hundred years, is that knowledge *grows*. It grows by leaps and bounds. Though we still do not know very much, it is just stunning how much more we know than our grandparents knew and how much more our grandchildren will know. Now given the sheer cumulative growth of knowledge, it seems to me a little bit silly to suppose that there is a *real* problem about whether knowledge is possible. In the seventeenth century when Descartes posed this question, they did not have a large body of universal, well established, objective knowledge. That was an era when the very possibility of universal, objective and certain knowledge was genuinely in question. (At that time for example many educated people believed in the existence of unicorns.) In the way that we can take the stock of knowledge—established knowledge—for granted, they could not. To see this stock of knowledge, go to any university bookstore and pick up elementary texts in such subjects as chemistry, biology or engineering. The sheer amount of established knowledge would have taken Descartes' breath away. For Descartes it was a *real* worry as to whether or not genuine scientific knowledge is possible? Now it is not a real worry, now it's a philosophical puzzle— *how* is it possible. But *that* it exists, that is not a real worry.

The situation is a bit like Zeno's paradoxes: it is a puzzle how I can cross the room if first I have to cross half, and before that half of that half, and so on. And it is a first rate philosophical exercise to solve Zeno's paradoxes, but nobody thinks that space does not exist on the basis of the paradoxes. We should have the same attitude to the skeptical paradoxes.

HRP: At the bottom of your philosophy there seems to be an assumption that we have some faculty of rationality or perception, that gives us access to an observer-independent reality.

Searle: Well I don't know that there is a *bottom*, but I think that the idea that somehow or other rationality is up for grabs makes no sense. A kid once said to me, "What is your argument for rationality?" Now think about that: the whole notion of an argument presupposes rationality.... Here is the point: rationality is not a separate thing, and it is not a separate faculty. It is wrong to think humans have a faculty of rationality. What humans have is mind and language. What they have is Intentional states and processes and the ability to perform speech acts. The constraints of rationality are *built in*—that is, you can't have a capacity for language or a capacity for thought without structural constraints of rationality. So rationality is not, so to speak, an *option*. The requirements of rationality are built into language and Intentionality. It is not some separate thing that you need to justify or that you can decide, "Well I'm going to have it or I won't have it." It is *built in as a set of structural constraints on talking and thinking*.

HRP: But those restraints actually do, you think, give us true knowledge? I mean couldn't they just be wired into our system wrong?

Searle: I think on occasion they give us true knowledge. To say that rationality is built in is not to say that most people are rational most of the time—that is not the point. But rather that there are constraints of rationality that are built into the structure of what people are thinking and saying. And of course sometimes they make systematic errors. As you know, Tversky and Kahnemann did these wonderful experiments where they got often very sophisticated professional people to make simple logical errors. So the fact that we have these constraints of rationality doesn't guarantee that we are going to talk and think rationally all or even most of the time. But I would not know what it would mean to say, "Maybe reasoning according to *modus ponens* is a massive trick that nature played on us, but it never in fact gives a valid result." I wouldn't know what that meant, because it is part of our conception of validity that if you have propositions of the form p and *if p, then q*, and you know that they are true, then you are entitled to infer q.

HRP: So something being valid just means that we're using rationality to figure it out.

Searle: As far as deductive arguments are concerned rationality defines validity. But that does not mean that irrationality is impossible. Of course it's possible; it's all too common. What is built in is not that you will win, but the rules of the game are built in. That is, what counts as rational and irrational is built in to the structure of thought and language. But of course that doesn't mean that people can't fail—they can and do.

HRP: So the concept of validity for you doesn't make any ontological claim about mind-independent reality, then?

Searle: No, these are separate points. There is a point about a mind-independent reality as a presupposition for thought and language, and then there is a structural feature of thought and language, namely that they come—like any game—with the rules of the game built in. So, just as football has the rules of football built into it, so thought and language have the rules of rationality built into it. I say that with some hesitation because—strictly speaking—the rules of rationality are not literally rules. They are, rather, built-in constraints. Arguments of the form p *and if p then q, therefore q* are not valid because they follow the rule of modus ponens, rather modus ponens is a valid rule because it articulates a pattern exemplified by an infinite number of arguments that are independently valid.

All of that, however, is separate from the point about direct realism in the philosophy of perception. This is a complex matter, but very crudely put there are two arguments for direct realism. First, the alternative has never been convincingly argued for or even coherently stated. All of the arguments I have ever seen to show that we do not perceive objects but only our own "sense data" are bad arguments. (See Austin's *Sense and Sensibilia* for a refutation of many of them) And second, as I remarked earlier, a public language presupposes a public world. But the publicity of that world is not just an ontological feature–that there really exist objects independent of us–but it has epistemic consequences. We have to have access to public objects if our discourse in a public language is to be intelligible and our access is primarily perceptual. However these are only hints and there is much more to be said.

THE LIMITS OF SCIENCE AND THE URGE TO PHILOSOPHY

HRP: Let's move on to your idea that philosophy starts from science, or from the basic facts of science. Would you say that that's a naturalistic approach to philosophy?

Searle: Well it is, but when I say "philosophy starts from the facts of science," that's a little bit misleading because it suggests that it is a sort of timeless prescription for philosophy and I don't mean it that way. What I mean is, *right now* at this stage in the history of intellectual life, as I said earlier, skepticism can't have the meaning for us that it had in the seventeenth century. There is a sense in which we can't take it seriously — we know too much. It is ridiculous for a guy to buy his airplane ticket, get on the airplane, work on his laptop, get off the plane, go give his lecture, and say in the lecture: "We don't know anything, there are only texts, but we have no knowledge of a reality outside of texts" — that's the deconstructionist confusion. But now we are at a particular phase in intellectual history. In the seventeenth century when Descartes posed his skeptical question, they did not have a large body of knowledge. That was an era when, as I remarked earlier, the possibility of universal, objective, and certain knowledge was in question.

HRP: Now it's not whether we can have knowledge, but what is the status of that knowledge — whether it has correspondence to some independent reality.

Searle: To grant that it is knowledge is already to grant the "correspondence." Thus if I know that snow is white, then snow is white. That is, in such cases, the knowledge, which is in my head, logically implies the existence of facts in the world, which are not in my head.

HRP: Do you think that our experiences will be entirely described or explained—and that the work of philosophy will be finished—once we have reconciled them with physics and chemistry?

Searle: Philosophy will never be finished. There will always be lots more. We are so smug about how much we know, but even given the growth of knowledge, our area of knowledge remains pathetically small. For example, I buy and read books about the brain: But we really do not know much about how the brain works. There are lots of philosophical problems that come out of the brain research. Furthermore, if you look at the history of philosophy, if you go back to the Greeks, and you think of the problems that bothered Greek philosophers, many of them are left unanswered by the sort of progress we have made. Even when my current problems are solved, many of the traditional problems are still going to be with us....

HRP: So you don't think the scientific reality can explain everything?

Searle: No, I think it is a terrible mistake to suppose that all of our hard philosophical questions have a scientific solution—most of them don't. Science has been good for giving us a little understanding of certain areas, but a lot of the most basic questions that bothered the Greek philosophers are beyond the reach of those methods: What is the good life? What is the good society? What is the nature of justice? I don't think they have a scientific answer. There are a *few* that we can hammer into shape, a few traditional philosophical questions like: What is life? That has pretty much been answered. And, What is consciousness? Or, How does the brain cause consciousness? That's a question that I hope we'll be able to answer.

HRP: What if appealing to the basic reality can't explain free will and can't answer questions like: What does it mean to be human? What should we do? What's meaningful in our lives? and so on. Do these missing or inexplicable aspects of our phenomenology pose a problem to your overall unified account of reality?

Searle: Even if I am successful there will still remain many unanswered questions. If I could get an answer to the questions that really bother me, I would feel that that was a pretty good day's work. Of course I would like to have a theory of justice as well—but then, Jack Rawls made impressive progress on that problem. So we can have some division of philosophical labor. We often have the feeling that you can't solve any philosophical problem until you solve them all. But there is a modified version of that, which says that there are a very large number of problems that hang together, and that there are going to be systematic relationships between your theory of mind and your theory of language and your theory of society and your theory of rationality—that has been my experience. How far does the systematicity go? I just don't know—we have to keep working on it. So, just to take something I'm working on now, if you go back and look at the great founders of social science, thinkers such as Durkheim, Weber, and Simmel, it seems to me that they could not *possibly* address their questions about the foundations of society adequately, because they had no theory of language. They took language for granted. Think about it: you want a theory of the fundamental ontology of human society. But if you assume that all these people already talk to each other in full blown human languages, then you have already *got* society because the practices of performing speech acts bring social reality along with them. I want to know: What exactly is the role of language in constituting society? That is a *fundamental* question neglected by the great classical social philosophers. More recent theorists like Bourdieu and Habermas think they are describing the role of language in the constitution of society. But in my view they do not succeed because (in their different ways) they have an inadequate theory of language and speech acts.

HRP: Apart from your project, what do you think is the aim of philosophy more generally? Do you think there is a more primordial motivation for doing philosophy?

Searle: Well I think that for a certain type of human intellect, philosophy is inevitable. Once you start a certain style of thinking you are bound to start reflecting on your most fundamental assumptions and presuppositions, and on absolutely general questions about how human beings fit in with the rest of the world, and how we relate to reality. I think the urge to philosophy is not something that is going to go away. We would of course like a scientific fix—we would like a scientific solution to our problems. And sometimes we get it, but there are a lot of things for which science hasn't even begun to give us a way of approaching questions. I mean the kinds of stuff that worry me about social ontology—that's not a question for physics and chemistry, that's a question of logical analysis. So I think philosophy is, literally, endless— that it will continue on. Now of course, horrible things might happen, maybe human beings will die out, but as long as there is a certain kind of intellect, there will be a certain set of questions. And it is one of the wonderful things about the Western intellectual tradition that the Greeks gave us systematic ways of thinking about these questions. And it really is quite unique; as far as I know there isn't anything quite like it in other civilizations. Other civilizations are wonderful and culturally advanced, but as far as I know there is nothing quite like the tradition that goes back to the pre-Socratics. Probably the most important invention of the Greeks was the idea of a theory, the idea of a systematic, logically related set of propositions that explain a domain.

The Greeks, by the way, had almost everything. They had the idea of a systematic theory, even an axiomatized theory. But they never got the idea of testing theory with experiments. The idea of an experimental natural philosophy only really comes with the Renaissance and after.

HRP: What does it feel like when you're working on a new problem in philosophy? You have really strong views on a lot of topics, and it seems like you're able to organize a lot of your thoughts in many different areas.

Searle: Well there isn't any single way that it feels like. I love working on philosophy. But I have to tell you, sometimes I have a feeling like...I get up in the morning and I run as hard as I can and bang my head against a brick wall. And I keep doing it until I make a hole in the wall, and you can sure get some headaches along the way. So it's not easy for me. I try to write *clearly*, and that gives people the impression that I find philosophy easy. No, it's *enormously* difficult to make it look easy! It's backbreaking labor to make complex matter simple enough so that you can convey it to your students and to the readers of your books. So people often have the impression that somehow I find philosophy easy. Not at all—it's devilishly hard.

HRP: There's something that struck me when I read an interview that we did with John Rawls some years back.[1] He commented that...well I can read the quote: "I'm a monomaniac, really. I like to get something right. But in philosophy one can't do that, not with any confidence. Real difficulties always remain." What do you think of that—do you think you can get things right?

Searle: I think there are some things you can get right. But I know what he's talking about: Once you really are confident that you have got something right, what you discover is that it opens up a whole new area of questions that you hadn't even been thinking about before. So to take a very simple case: the idea that you are going to duplicate consciousness simply by writing a computer program. I can show it is wrong. But once you *see* that that is wrong, you have still got a whole lot of questions: What *is* the nature of computation? How *does* it relate to the biological processes of human mental life? So if you answer one question, you find that it opens up a whole bunch of questions.... That quotation, by the way, is terrific; that is typical Jack. I love that.

THE MIND-BODY PROBLEM

HRP: I wanted to touch on the mind-body problem, and get that on the table. You spend a good amount of time talking about it—what's the main problem, the main question that people are trying to solve here?

Searle: [chuckles]...This is one of those wonderful problems in philosophy where you can see how people get *hung up* on assumptions that they never question. Here is why there is a problem. If you pinch yourself, you have this experience, and it has got all these apparently mysterious features—it is qualitative, it is subjective, and it is private in the sense that I stand in a relation to my pain, that you don't stand to my pain. That gives you a model for what the mental is like. Then you look around, and you see that the world is made of physical objects, and you know they are made of molecules, and suddenly you get this horrible worry: How can this subjective, qualitative, private mental stuff—how can *that* exist, in a world of physical objects? How can it be caused by material processes? And once you have got that, then the problem is off and *running*. You see, the problem now as I stated it is wrongly put. But this is how it is commonly put. I have been reading a bunch of textbooks on the philosophy of mind, because I am supposed to *write* one myself and I thought I ought to read the others first. They all make the same mistake: they all assume that somehow or other the mental qua mental can't be physical qua physical, so that this naïve conception of the mental and the physical *already* implies mutual exclusion. And then the theorists have two ways they can jump, either dualism or materialism. The dualists say, "Well, you have to postulate a separate realm. You have to accept some version of dualism, such as dual aspect theory, substance dualism (rare nowadays) or property dualism." The materialists say, "No, it's all an illusion. There aren't any intrinsic and irreducible Intentional states or conscious states. The belief in the irreducibly mental is just an illusion because mental phenomena can be reduced to 'something else'." And then follows their favorite version of materialism. In recent decades the favorite candidates for the fundamental materialist ontology to which the mind can be reduced are behavior, computer programs, brain states as neurobiologically described, and functional states of the organism. Reductionists like to think they are different from eliminativists. The eliminativists say mental states do not really exist. Reductionists say they really exist but are really something else. But both at bottom are the same. They both reject the view that the world contains states and processes that are intrinsically and irreducibly subjective, qualitative, private and often intentional. So what is the way out? I want to say, *go back* and look at the basic assumption you are all making. The most basic assumption is that the mental, naïvely construed, is somehow or other different from, and exclusive of, the material, naively construed. Now I want to say, if you see them correctly, if you see mental processes as biological phenomena going on in the brain, then the question "How does the mind relate to the brain?" is about like the question "How does digestion relate to the stomach?" Of course the relation of mental processes to the brain are in several ways unlike the relation of digestion to the stomach, because digestion does not have the first person or subjective ontology of mental phenomena. But basically, once you naturalize the problem, once you recognize mental phenomena as ordinary features of our biological existence, like digestion or mitosis, then you can both recognize the obvious truth about conscious states—that they are qualitative, subjective, internal, private, and have Intentionality in many cases—and at the same time recognize that the world consists entirely of physical particles. So what we are talking about is a biological process. That's the basic solution to the mind-body problem. Then you have to go on and say a whole lot more about it—you have to answer questions about mental causation, for example, or about Intentionality. But if you look at the standard literature [chuckle/gasp], you find it is quite *stunning* because the theorists locked in the traditional categories find obvious facts to be impossible: "How can it ever be the case," [dramatic tone of mock wonderment and desperation] "that my conscious thought should cause my arm to go up, when my arm going up is an event in the physical world! and my conscious thought is an event in the mental world!?" That whole way of looking at the matter, I believe, is wrong. And here I will steal an argument from you and give your example about the water carving the sides of the Grand Canyon. It seems to be a beautiful example, exactly the sort of thing I am talking about....

HRP: Because you have two levels of description....

Searle: Exactly, you have a micro level and a macro level. You can say that neuron firings are causing my arm to go up—that is certainly true. Or you can say that my conscious decision is causing my arm to go up. Just as you can say that the zillions of H_2O molecules are moving the minute particles of the sides of the canyon. Or you can say *rushing water* is *tearing away* at the walls of the canyon. There is no causal over-determination, there is no problem about a higher level (that is, there is no epiphenomenalism), it is just a typical case where you have different levels of description of the same causal system.

HRP: Yeah, I do think you definitely...

Searle: By the way, I *honestly* think our view is going to prevail. That is, I think in a hundred years' time, people will rub their eyes in disbelief to think, "This was a big-deal problem at the beginning of the twenty-first century?"

HRP: Is it important to you to try to convince other people now?

Searle: Well, life is only so long. Of course, one would like to convince people now, but it's not urgent. When I first wrote *Speech Acts*, a lot of people assured me, "That's not really philosophy. That's linguistics." And linguists said, "No, no, whatever it is, it is not linguistics." But in the end they come around. If you don't believe that truth has a chance of prevailing, you shouldn't be in this profession. I think it will prevail.

HRP: So that was pretty much the answer to the question of how it's *possible* for consciousness to exist in a physical world, and that's not really a problem.

Searle: I don't see that as a problem. I think there is an interesting and difficult neurobiological problem: How the does the brain do it? And we really don't understand that. We are not even sure what the right level of description is.

HRP: And are these the only problems, the only questions, that we can ask about consciousness?

Searle: Of course not. I divide the questions into two parts: There are the "big deal" problems that are supposed to be brain-breakers for philosophers; and then there are a whole lot of questions which *to me* are *just* as fascinating: How does it really work in real life? Now there are three brain-breaking questions in this mind-body area, and they are: 1) How is it possible for the brain to cause consciousness? 2) How can mental events ever cause physical events? and 3) How can there ever be such a thing as Intentionality? How can the mind reach *beyond* itself to objects, and states of affairs in the world? And if you look at the standard textbooks, that is mostly what they are about. But for me, there are in addition many—in a sense just as interesting, maybe more interesting— questions, namely: What is consciousness anyway? What are its main features, and how do they relate to each other? And about Intentionality: How does it work in detail? People say "beliefs, desires, et cetera"—but what is this "et cetera"? What is the relation between beliefs and desires? What is the formal structure of Intentionality? Frankly, to me, those questions become *more* interesting than the basic question. Once you see the general solution to the basic questions, then you still have these *fascinating* questions left over. It is not, How is meaning possible at all? But, What is the structure of speech acts? How many kinds are there, and how do they relate to each other? So I am as much interested—and right now more interested—in specific detailed questions of the form, How does it work in fact? than in big metaphysical questions about how such a thing is possible at all.

PHENOMENOLOGY AND ITS PROPONENTS

HRP: Let's go to that. A lot of your work describes the structure of consciousness, and almost just *observes* it, and turns out what you observe about it—you know, the 'periphery' and the *way* that consciousness appears to us.

Searle: You would be surprised how few philosophers are willing to do that. Most of them are not *interested* in that. They think, "No, we want to get to the *mind-body* problem as quickly as we can." But I would like to know: If you start listing the features of consciousness, how many can you come up with? And it gets to be quite a list. And again with Intentionality, there is the "big-deal" question of how the mind can *reach out* to objects so far away. But once you see the general outline of the solution to that, then you can ask, What is a *taxonomy* of Intentional states? How do they relate to each other? I try to do that, with the distinction between the 'cognitive' and the 'volitive', and the different 'directions of fit' and different directions of causation.

HRP: It seems like a lot of your descriptions of the structure of consciousness are phenomenological descriptions—you are basically talking about how it seems to us, when we're conscious. But then elsewhere you seem to be describing something different—a reality that is not present to our experience.

Searle: That is a very good point. You see, I said earlier: use any methodology, use any method that comes to hand. Now, one way to start is phenomenologically, to describe how your conscious experiences seem to you—What kind of experiences do you have? But for me phenomenology is only the beginning, because there is a whole area that is beyond the reach of phenomenological analysis. That is the area where the main question is: What is the logical structure? And many of the questions about logical structure have no phenomenological reality. That is, you discover when you analyze memory that it has a causal condition, because unless the event you think you remember actually caused your memory, then you don't really remember it. But there is typically no phenomenology to the causal condition on memory. You don't *sense* the event *forcing* you to the memory—maybe you do in odd cases, but not in most cases; there's no phenomenological reality. So, the answer to this question is: Use the phenomenology to begin with, but don't stop when you run out of phenomenological gas. Now, I cannot tell you how important that is. Because a lot of my critics—and I didn't discover this until much later—think I'm trying to do phenomenology. And they point out, there's no phenomenological reality to what you say, so they think, it cannot be real. But that doesn't follow, because of course the phenomenology only reaches so far. By the way—I couldn't believe it—a lot of people thought I was trying to be like Husserl, or something like that. I can't *imagine* a philosopher further from me in methodology than Husserl. His method was just to describe the structure of his experience after he made the phenomenological reduction. What I'm trying to do is describe the 'conditions of satisfaction' whether they're phenomenologically real or not.

HRP: You say that phenomenology only reaches so far. But let me make sure I have this right: Phenomenology is simply that which describes our human reality, so it seems to me that it would be very important for

you to take phenomenology seriously and to fully describe our human reality before reconciling it with the scientific reality....

Searle: Of course. The problem is that traditionally phenomenologists describe only the features of the human reality that are phenomenologically available. And indeed, my objection to the phenomenologists is that they do not examine the human reality right. They don't get the right set of relationships between the human reality and the fundamental reality, and many of them are unable to pose and answer the questions. So, for example, I have a question in social ontology that goes: What are the relationships between the brute physical reality of atoms and electrons and molecules, and the social and institutional reality of money and property and marriage and government? Now, the problem I have with phenomenologists is that they can't hear that question at all or they don't hear it in the right way. Either with Husserl, they take it as a question about transcendental consciousness, and they think it must be a question about how we Intentionally first construe something as a brute physical fact, and then convert it into an institutional fact—that's wrong. Or with the Heideggerians, they think that somehow or other Dasein is primary, and the basic reality of physics is somehow a privation or a subtraction from Dasein.

They think that when I talk about the brute physical reality of atoms and molecules I must be adopting a "detached third person stance" or some such. They cannot hear the question, or hear the answer that I am giving to this question—and I have this problem with [Hubert] Dreyfus. Dreyfus literally cannot understand my project: he thinks it must be either Husserl or Heidegger, and it's neither, it is not like either of them.

HRP: Tell me how it's not like Husserl.

Searle: Asking how my views are not like Husserl is like asking me how they are not like St. Thomas Aquinas. I operate in a totally different logical space from either Husserl or Heidegger (or for that matter Aquinas).

I am no expert on these philosophers but this is one way they are standardly interpreted. Neither Husserl nor Heidegger can start where I start, nor pose the questions that I pose. They can't start with atomic physics and evolutionary biology and see the human reality as derivative from these more fundamental parts of the real world. Husserl starts with the transcendental ego and the transcendental reduction and he tries to provide foundations for knowledge. All of this is foreign to my whole way of thinking. Heidegger starts with the primordiality of Dasein. Both are starting on the wrong foot. If you start with atomic physics and evolutionary biology then you begin your investigation by recognizing that all mental phenomena are caused by brain processes and realized in the brain. And if, for example, the transcendental ego or Dasein really existed they would have to be parts of our biology, like any other. They would have be realized in neurobiological processes in the brain, presumably in the thalamorcortical system. Such a way of thinking, though obvious to me, is utterly alien to Husserl and Heidegger.

When we get to my conception of social reality the differences become even greater. For me the crucial question is how do human minds impose institutional status functions on objects and people in the world. For example, how do we get from the bits of paper to dollar bills, how do we get from the sounds that come out of my mouth to speech acts? Now phenomenologists typically cannot hear that question and they cannot hear the answer, because they have an impoverished philosophical apparatus. They think I am asking a phenomenological question, because they have no other apparatus to deal with the question. They think I am asking, How does it seem to us? But typically how it seems to us does not reveal the underlying logical structure. Thus Husserlians suppose that we create institutional facts by first identifying something as meaningless and then intentionally imposing meaning on it. But except in odd cases that is wrong. For example, the kid just grows up using money. So the Husserlians give a false answer because they did not understand the question. They took it as a phenomenological question, when it is in fact about logical structure. The Heideggerians are worse. They think the question dissolves, because from a phenomenological point of view, we don't phenomenologically experience ourselves imposing status functions. The bits of paper are "always already" money, the spoken sounds we hear are "always already" speech acts. (By the way, when these guys say "always already," reach for your gun.) Both commit what I call the phenomenological fallacy of assuming that what is not phenomenologically real is not real, that what structure is not phenomenologically available, is not real structure. The Husserlians see that there is a logical structure, but mistakenly locate it in the phenomenology. The Heideggerians see that it is not in the phenomenology so they deny that there is any logical structure. Both are committing the phenomenological fallacy.

We know even before doing philosophy that there must be an *answer* to such questions as, What is the relationship between the piece of paper and the money? And, What is the relation between the sounds and the speech act? Because initially, at least, we know in advance that the relationship is one of identity; this piece of paper just *is* money. These sounds just *are* a speech act. Because of its failure to start with the basic facts of physics and biology and because of it impoverished methodology, phenomenology cannot pose the right questions or hear the answers when they are given.

So the difference between me and Husserl (and Heidegger) is that I found them both to proceed from false assumptions, using an impoverished methodology.

LOGICAL ANALYSIS

HRP: You call your analysis of intentional[2] action in terms of conditions of satisfaction a logical analysis rather then a phenomenological one. Why do you use the term 'logical conditions'? What do you mean by "logical"?

Searle: Logic in general is a matter of logical relations, such as entailment, validity, and truth, between propositions and other semantic entities and facts and states of affairs in the world. The Intentional contents of beliefs, desires, intentions, and so on are propositional, so they stand in logical relations to each other and have truth conditions or other sorts of conditions of satisfaction, by which they relate to facts and states of affairs in the world.

Anything that can succeed or fail has conditions of success or failure. Now, conditions are always propositional in nature. It is always *that* such and such is the condition. So there always has to be a condition *that such and such* that states the condition of satisfaction. All of that is a matter of logical relations. But it's important to see that none of that—what I just told you—is supposed to be phenomenological. If you have the belief that it is raining, you need not be always consciously thinking, "I believe it is raining," but all the same your belief has conditions of satisfaction, in this case truth conditions. When you *unpack* the *structure* of Intentional phenomena, what you find are conditions of success and failure, and those conditions will be stated propositionally. But of course, in many cases, there is no phenomenological reality to these propositions—why should there be?

HRP: If this logical structure has nothing to do with our phenomenology, how do you argue that conditions of satisfaction are essential to, or constitutive of, our actions?

Searle: I don't say logical structure has nothing to do with phenomenology, but rather that phenomenology is not enough to uncover all the logical structures. You need the notion of conditions of satisfaction, because without them you can't distinguish between succeeding and failing. And you can't distinguish between those cases where something happens to you that *has no* conditions of succeeding or failing—if you fall off a building or hiccup—and going for a walk, which *does* have conditions of satisfaction.

HRP: Those distinctions are real phenomenological distinctions we make. It sounds like you're really saying that success and failure are essential to a certain subset of our conscious experiences: the experiences of trying to do something.

Searle: It is not just a matter of consciously trying to do things, but rather

of all intentionality, conscious or unconscious, and whether
intentionality in action, perception, thoughts, memory, feelings, emotions,
or speaking. In general, as you go through your life you are having mental
states, conscious or unconscious. For example, you can be doing something
or experiencing something, or thinking about something, or all of these.
We need to describe what the structure is by which these experiences—
action, perception, thought, speaking, or whatever—relate to the rest of
the world: the short answer is conditions of satisfaction.

The real bankruptcy of phenomenology as traditionally practiced
comes out in the theory of descriptions. What does the phenomenologist
say about an utterance of "The King of France is bald?" The Russellian
analysis is simply beyond the reach of Hussserl, Heidegger, or Merleau-
Ponty because the conditions of satisfaction (in this case truth conditions)
are not phenomenologically realized in the consciousness of the speaking
agent. But why should they be?

**HRP: Let's take an example. When you're doing something, any kind of
intentional action—skiing, let's say, which you do a lot—you ski down
a mountain and make a turn, and you say there's an 'intention-in-action',
and there are conditions of satisfaction, when you do that.**

Searle: Absolutely. And you can see it phenomenologically. If you ask
yourself...

HRP: *Sometimes*, right?

Searle: If you are actually skiing, not just sometimes, but almost always.
It is funny that you picked skiing as the example, because *there* the
conscious experience is what it is *all about*. I mean, skiing is not like
shaving or hammering nails. It's something you do precisely because of
the character of the phenomenological experience. Ask yourself, What
would it be like if when I skied it was like the Wilder Penfield cases (*The
Mystery of the Mind*) where Penfield produces a bodily movement by
stimulating the motor cortex? Now imagine that some scientist from
another planet is entirely directing my skiing by controlling my brain
with a science fiction type of ray gun. In such a case I won't feel myself
making any turns at all. I would feel my body being moved down the
mountain, entirely independently of my will. There would be no
Intentionality except for that of my observations of what is happening
to me. But that is not what it is normally like to ski. What it's like to ski
is to have a sense at all times of alternate possibilities open and to have
a sense of deciding what you're going to do and then carrying out your
intentions by doing it.

But that's not the key point. The key point is a logical point. What
counts as succeeding or failing? What counts as doing what you were
trying to do, as actually succeeding in the enterprise that you undertook?
The answers to those questions will reveal the conditions of satisfaction.

So the argument for the distinction between the 'prior intention' and the intention-in-action is that you can have one without the other: you can have a prior intention without doing anything, or you can do something spontaneously, without a prior plan to do it. But the argument that when you're actually carrying out a process—what I call the "flow," as in the flow of intentional behavior skiing down a mountain—you can't explain that without recognizing the *fact* that there are these intentions-in-action; that you are doing the act intentionally. There are a number of arguments for the need to introduce conditions of satisfaction into the account, but the basic one is that wherever you can succeed or fail, you have conditions of success and failure, and those are what I call conditions of satisfaction.

HRP: Right. But you think the success and failure are actually *part* of the experience, part of the phenomenology?

Searle: When you are engaged in a concentrated conscious activity such as skiing the conditions of success and failure are *built in* to the conscious experience. For example when you fall down, you typically feel like an idiot because you know you should not have fallen there. Then the conditions of satisfaction of your intention-in-action have failed; because that's not what you were trying to do.

But skiing is unusual in that the whole point of doing it is to experience the conscious phenomenology. But there are lots of other activities, such as driving to work or walking across the campus to class, which are also intentional, with conditions of satisfaction, but where the phenomenology of the experience is secondary, and indeed many Intentional aspects of the experience may be unconscious.

HRP: So you wouldn't want to say that having this sense of failure is characteristic of all intentional actions?

Searle: The expression, "sense of failure" is already too phenomenological. The point is that all intentionality, whether in thought, language, action, perception or memory can succeed or fail. If it can succeed or fail it has conditions of success and failure and these are, trivially, propositional, because the notion of a condition is always a condition that such and such. It is always propositional. But the agent need not have a prior conscious "sense of failure." It is no accident that there is no serious, well worked out theory of language in the phenomenological tradition, because the important points in the theory of speech acts, or in other contemporary semantic theories, are beyond the reach of phenomenological analysis.

HRP: What about an action like exploring, where you don't have a clear goal, a clear sense of what would count as succeeding? If I'm exploring a new area, there's not really any success or failure involved; you succeed

just by doing it.

Searle: Well you just stated the goal. It is "exploring a new area." And in achieving that goal you will presumably have lots of subsidiary goals, like "climbing this hill and looking at the view." Conditions of satisfaction can be as vague and indeterminate as the Intentional state in question, because they are the content of that very state.

Sometimes you have conditions of satisfaction where you do not know in advance what it will feel like when they are satisfied. Thus, for example, when you're skiing, you always try to make perfect turns, and you know that the turn is getting better, because you feel it, but you don't know what it's going to feel like before it happens, and you don't know exactly what the perfect turn is going to feel like prior to having made it. So you don't have to know in advance what it's going to feel like, but you do have to be trying to improve yourself. And that has conditions of satisfaction. But now, I'm not sure what other kind of case you had in mind. I just go for a walk in the countryside, and I have no particular objective to the walk, but that's fine. That's a case where that *was* my objective, to have a walk in the countryside.

HRP: Okay, so then you don't see doing things absent-mindedly as fundamentally different from doing things consciously (in the flow)? I mean, you think they're both experiences of trying to do something?

Searle: Yes, but I want to be sure that when you say "experiences" you are not confining yourself to conscious experiences. Sure, there are lots of things you do unreflectively, but still intentionally. For example, in a philosophical discussion like this, I typically get up and walk around. In such cases I don't first sit here thinking, "I'm going to get up and walk around." No, it's just perfectly natural for me to get up and walk around. And in this case I am walking around talking about walking around. But of course all of this is intentional behavior. It all has conditions of satisfaction.

HRP: So it has the same structure as behavior that I'm conscious about has?

Searle: Yes, and the proof of that is that you can bring it to consciousness at any moment.

HRP: Exactly, so your logical conditions essentially all come down to either potential or actual *flow*, and how that works.

Searle: There are three serious qualifications you have to make to that. First not all intentional actions are part of a "flow." You can ski down a mountain in a flow of intentional action, but you can't write the *Critique of Pure Reason* in a flow. Second, action is only one kind of case. Don't forget that the analysis of Intentionality applies to belief, memory, perception, desire, fear, and lots of other cases. And third, remember also that the "flow" can be either conscious or unconscious.

HRP: When you say that a lot of your logical analysis doesn't have any phenomenological reality, that position sounds kind of parallel to me to your 'deep unconscious' argument. You criticize people who believe in the deep unconscious for saying that we follow unconscious rules that don't have any phenomenological reality. Couldn't they just mean "rules" almost metaphorically? That is, *logically* you can say there are rules, but they're not real in terms of phenomenology?

Searle: No, the two cases are different, you see, because the deep unconscious theorists want to invoke the apparatus of rule-governed behavior. And I point out that, with the deep unconscious, you cannot have that apparatus, because you don't have intentional causation. And why don't you have intentional causation? Because the putative rules don't have what I call 'aspectual shape'; they don't have what Frege called a 'mode of presentation'.

HRP: But that's a phenomenological thing.

Searle: Not actually but only potentially. The mode of presentation needn't be present to consciousness at every moment, but it's got to be the kind of thing that *could in principle* become conscious. Similarly with my conditions of satisfaction, you *can* become conscious of what you are trying to do. You can focus your attention on what you are trying to do—on the conditions of succeeding and failing. But often you're not thinking about it at all. I gave you the example of driving a car: there are conditions of satisfaction of driving a car, even though my attention might be elsewhere—I might be thinking about a philosophical problem. But notice that at *any instant* I can switch my attention back to focus on my driving.

HRP: So then conditions of satisfaction are *potentially* conscious, and that's the difference from the unconscious.

Searle: That's right. One and the same intentional content can be either conscious or unconscious.

HRP: Or in other words, your logical analysis is essentially phenomenological in kind: I mean, it is a description of what intentional action means *to us*, since you get the conditions of satisfaction by asking yourself how it seems to you.

Searle: No, not by asking how it consciously seems to you but by asking yourself, What would we say if...? That is, How would our concepts apply under such-and-such conditions? You don't just introspect what it feels like. You can't just ask, What does it feel like to raise my arm? But you ask, Under what conditions would I say I had succeeded or failed in what I was trying to do?

HRP: Right. But then phenomenology is not really the same as introspectionism. Your logical analysis is still some kind of description of how it works for us.

Searle: Of course, how it works for conscious beings. Even though many of the phenomena are not conscious and thus have no phenomenological reality at the time of the experience and many of the logical features are unavailable to phenomenology, even when conscious.

THE LATER WITTGENSTEIN

HRP: What do you think of the later Wittgenstein?

Searle: Well, my gosh. Wittgenstein is the one philosopher in my life whose works I actually tried to master. The *Philosophical Investigations* was published when I first started doing philosophy seriously, and I virtually memorized the book. I really worked on it, and in fact I nagged many of my teachers to discuss it with me. I got Austin to hold sessions with his undergraduate class about the *Investigations*. Austin hated it, he just thought it was hopelessly confused. Austin made a point of interpreting everything absolutely literally. He was somewhat ironical, but he once said: "Alright, next week, everyone has to bring a box with a beetle in it." Well, we didn't of course bring such a box, but then Austin would say: "Wittgenstein says everyone has something in his box—we'll call it a beetle—and then later he turns around and says, perhaps there's nothing in the box! A plain self-contradiction!" Austin thought he had discovered that Wittgenstein was just sloppy, just loose. This is a digression, but the point is that I did at one time try to learn Wittgenstein's later work very carefully, and I read all that intermediate stuff—the *Blue Book* and *Brown Book* and so on, as well as, of course, the *Tractatus* and then post-*Investigations* stuff like the *Reflections on the Foundations of Mathematics* and *On Certainty*. Of the so-called great philosophers, the one I know best is Wittgenstein.

However having said that, I would also have to add that I was fully aware by the time I was writing *Speech Acts* that the kind of philosophy I do is a kind that Wittgenstein would have hated, because it attempts to be systematic and theoretical. I don't just "assemble reminders for a purpose" or "describe language games," I want to develop a theory. Now there is a certain irony, and that is: I think Wittgenstein paved the way for a kind of philosophy he would have abominated. I think he helped make the kind of thing I do possible, but he would have hated the kind of thing I do. And the way that he helped make it possible was essentially to remove certain types of philosophical skepticism from the agenda. That is, he showed that—in addition to this other stuff I was telling you about, the sheer growth of knowledge—he showed that we really can't take skepticism seriously in a way that philosophers in the past thought they could take it seriously. And so by removing that from the agenda—this analogy just occurred to me, I don't know if it's a good one—in the way that Mrs. Thatcher removed socialism from the agenda of British politics and thus made it possible for labor party types like Tony Blair to be pro-capitalist, so Wittgenstein removed a certain type of skepticism, a certain way of approaching epistemology, from the philosophical agenda and thus made it possible for systematic theoreticians like me to flourish.

HRP: So you don't see your analysis as merely description.

Searle: I want a theory, I want a theoretical account of whole domains, such as speech acts, Intentionality, social ontology, and rationality.

HRP: Do you think that words have meanings floating around as these logical objects, apart from their actual use in practice?

Searle: Well there I am with Wittgenstein: meaning is not the name of an introspective entity, it is not the name of a kind of thought-process, it is not a little picture that you carry around in your head. But, roughly speaking, to know the meaning of a word is to have a certain ability to use that word in Intentional behavior, to form sentences and to apply the word truly or falsely. I think Wittgenstein's attack on the introspectionist account of meaning is quite correct. I agree with it. But a lot of people interpret it behavioristically—I do not. I am not a behaviorist. That is, they say: "Well look, if the computer can answer questions then it must know the meaning of all the words." No, it doesn't. That conclusion does not follow. So I do not interpret the slogan "meaning is use" behavioristically.

HRP: So the meaning of a word is either a description of all the ways we use it, or it's an ability to know how to use it in those various ways.

Searle: Beware of sentences that begin "the meaning of a word is..." and think rather of sentences such as: "When one learns the meaning of a word one learns..." and part of the end of the sentence is "how to use the word in speaking." The point is: the ability to use a word is the ability to engage in Intentionalistic human conscious behavior with the word. Using the word is not just an event that happens in the world independent of our Intentionality.

HRP: And similarly with actions: Apart from describing what actually characterizes those actions in practice, do you think they have a

particular structure with necessary and sufficient conditions?

Searle: Well, the notion of necessary and sufficient conditions is always tricky, because one can often find exceptions to analyses in terms of necessary and sufficient conditions. But the idea that Intentional human behavior has a logical structure is something that I absolutely agree to; it must have a logical structure because it has propositional content, and those propositional contents have a logical structure. Now where I think I go beyond a lot of people is that I think that what we think of as social reality—human social reality—also has a logical structure, because propositional contents of representations are partly constitutive of the structure, and you can give a logical analysis of those propositional contents. That's what *The Construction of Social Reality* is all about—it's about the logical structure of society.

HRP: You know, I think when you say "logical structure" you don't mean what other people hear when they hear it.

Searle: What do they hear? That logical structure must imply an axiomatic system?

HRP: Or some kind of underlying metaphysical space...coming from some privileged viewpoint outside ourselves...

Searle: Yes, but it doesn't mean that. The logical structure of society is revealed by the set of propositions that are partly constitutive of society.

HRP: And I think it might be closer to phenomenology than it seems to people, broadly defined as the study of our human reality.

Searle: Perhaps some ideal phenomenology, but not phenomenology as it is actually practiced. As practiced it is very limited, and when it comes to the questions that interest me it is largely bankrupt, because many of the logical structures are not phenomenologically available. As I said earlier, with the example of the theory of descriptions, in general the logical relations are beyond the reach of phenomenology. Heidegger says that stating is like pointing. I am afraid that is not much help. And as I tried to point out earlier, the logical structure of money, marriage, and government is for the most part beyond the reach of phenomenological analysis.

HRP: I asked you why you thought conditions of satisfaction are essential to consciousness, and you said that without them you couldn't distinguish between succeeding and failing, or between something that happens to you versus something you *do*—and those are, you know, things that we experience, things that we actually do distinguish for ourselves.

Searle: Exactly, absolutely. If the word hadn't already been corrupted, I would call myself a phenomenologist, at least as far as the beginning of logical investigations are concerned. You begin with how things seem to you. Phenomenology can be the *beginning* of the investigation. It just does not go very far.

HRP: Maybe you could comment on what you meant when you wrote (in *Intentionality*) that: "There is no non-intentional standpoint from which we can survey the relations between Intentional states and their conditions of satisfaction. Any analysis must take place from within the circle of Intentional concepts."[3] This seems like an important clarification.

Searle: This is a very difficult issue, and I will have to be very brief. Think of it this way, there is no non-linguistic standpoint from which we can survey the relations between language and reality to see if language is adequate to reality because any such surveying we do would have to be done in a language. Similarly, there is no non-logical standpoint from which we can survey the adequacy of logic because any such surveying would have to be done within the constraints of logic. What these examples reveal is simply less general forms of the completely general statement that there is no non-Intentional standpoint from which we can survey the relationship between Intentional states and their conditions of satisfaction. Any such surveying has to be done using an Intentionalistic apparatus.

HOLISM AND THE BACKGROUND OF THOUGHT AND ACTION

HRP: One other point that I never asked you about: you say you're an internalist as opposed to an externalist. What views do you have that make you an internalist?

Searle: There are different questions to which internalism and externalism are answers. And one question—the original question that came up—was about meaning. The question is: Are the contents of the mind—or as people now would have to say the contents of the brain—sufficient to determine the meaning of words in a language? And I want to say yes, they are. And then it becomes a question of analyzing the arguments that are supposed to have shown decisively that the contents of the mind are *not* sufficient to determine the meanings. What I try to show is that those are not good arguments. The standard argument is that there is an indexical component in the conditions of satisfaction. And I grant that. I think there *is* typically an indexical component, but that is not something that is external to the mind; the indexical component, the indexical requirement, is *set by* the contents of the mind. So I agree with the externalists that the meaning of 'water' is not given by a checklist of general terms ("water is a clear, colorless, tasteless liquid"). You have to add some indexical component to the definition. But the requirement of an indexical component does not refute internalism, because the indexical component has to be internally represented, otherwise it is not going to function.

HRP: What about the experience of consciousness? Some people would say that we're not totally self-contained in our mental world, that there's a lot of interaction with the outside world that is a primary part of our phenomenology, and that is logically necessary for us to experience consciousness as we do. What about that kind of externalism?

Searle: I am not quite sure what that one means.

HRP: You said that consciousness is essentially subjective. Do you want to say that it's *totally* subjective? Do you need to say that, or can you just say essentially subjective? Do you need a complete separation?

Searle: Always start with examples. I feel a pain. Now there are two kinds of subjectivity for me, there is the ontological and the epistemic. And the pain is ontologically subjective, because it only exists in so far as it is experienced by a subject, namely me. But if I have the conscious experience of seeing a tree, then my conscious experience will be satisfied only if there is actually a tree there. So the Intentionality of the perceptual experience represents actual objects in the world. But the conscious experience itself can exist even if it is a hallucination, even if it does not in fact give me access to objects in the world.

HRP: What if you were born without any external world—well, born in a dark room without any external stimulus. Would your mental life...

Searle: It would be very impoverished.

HRP: I guess I'm thinking about the background. The background is so much related to society and external stimuli, could it exist without the world?

Searle: Well you do have some features of the background that are innate. I am pretty confident about that—that the brain structures a lot of your consciousness. The disposition to walk on your hind legs or the capacity to learn language, those are abilities that are built in to the structure of the brain. But, of course, you have to be in a society and you have to be in contact with the external world to trigger those innate capacities and in order that you can have certain kinds of consciousness. But the conscious experiences nonetheless go on inside your skin. Here is an analogy: In order that you can have digestion, there has to be a whole food industry, there have to be farmers, and there have to be all sorts of ways of getting the food to the store and from the store to the table; but all the same, digestion goes on internally. It is not a complex relationship between you and the farmer. And similarly I want to say that in order that you can have the experience of reading books or going to the movies or learning philosophy, of course you have to be involved in society, but the actual impact of society is that it stimulates your nerve endings in such a way that you have conscious experiences inside your skin.

HRP: Sure. But it seems insufficient to say that the background is a set of physical abilities. Of course that is true, but what about the philosophical significance of it in terms of a holism that seems to connect us with a shared world? This isn't a physical thing, but it's the philosophical implication.

Searle: I agree with that.

HRP: Okay, so in that sense, you could say that we're not self-sufficient subjects or minds; there's a sense in which we are already logically connected with the world....

Searle: Of course. We are essentially social, and we are in a real world and our discourse only makes sense on the presupposition that we see ourselves as engaging with the real world. But it is still logically possible that I could have all of the mental phenomena I do have, including my background capacities, and still be radically mistaken. I could still be the proverbial "brain in a vat."

HRP: I think that's sort of what the "always already" thing is trying to get at—they're not trying to deny that of course we're *physically* self-contained, but they're saying that it's misleading to talk about us as subjects merely perceiving an external world.

Searle: Of course. But if that is the claim, they are attacking a straw person. The view of human life as consisting entirely of passive perceptions is not widely held and in fact, I am not sure anyone ever held it.

APPROACHES TO PHILOSOPHY

HRP: I wanted to talk more generally about what you think the difference is between analytic and Continental philosophy. Something Umberto Eco said in an interview with us a few years ago on his thoughts on that difference struck me, and I'm wondering what you think of it. He says:

> I think that analytical philosophy still has a medieval attitude: it seems that every discourse is expected to start from a previous one, everybody recognizing a sort of canon, let us say the Fregean one. In this line of thought one has to respect a common philosophical jargon, to start from a set of canonical

questions, and any new proposal must stem from that corpus of questions and answers. Continental philosophers try to show that they have nothing to do with the previous philosophical discourses, even when they are only translating old problems into a new philosophical language.[4]

Might that be a valid criticism of analytic philosophers, in terms of their reliance on the same canon of questions and types of problems?

Searle: I think Umberto is completely mistaken. When I wrote my book *The Construction of Social Reality*, there simply was no corpus of literature on the subject. Sometimes philosophers write in response to other philosophers, sometimes not. Similarly when I wrote *Speech Acts*, there was no huge corpus of work on the subject. I knew of Austin's lectures and literally nothing else. When I wrote *Intentionality*, there was a huge corpus of phenomenological work, but I simply ignored it, because it seemed so bad. It seems puzzling that Umberto should say this about analytic philosophy because one of the things that strikes analytic philosophers is how much Continental philosophy is about the same small list of proper names: Hegel, Nietzsche, Heidegger, Husserl, Merleau-Ponty, Kierkegaard, and a few others.

My guess is that Umberto was struck by the fact that analytic philosophy tends to be conversational in tone. That is, people write an article where they discuss other articles, so you have the impression that analytic philosophy is a kind of continuous, published conversation.

Actually, I am suspicious of the so-called distinction between analytic and Continental philosophy. You see, here's the irony for me. I am supposed to be an analytic philosopher—an Anglo-American philosopher. But I have taught courses at Frankfurt with Jürgen Habermas; we taught a seminar together. And he came to my seminars when he was in Berkeley. And nobody said, "Well you're an analytic philosopher and he's a Continental philosopher." I was invited by Pierre Bourdieu to give a series of lectures at the Collège de France. And who do I talk to when I am in France? Well, before he died, Michel Foucault. I have no problem with these guys, and nobody ever says, "Well you're an analytic philosopher and I'm a Continental philosopher." Or for that matter with Umberto—Umberto organized a thing for me in San Marino, we had a big one-day fest and a lot of people came and threw arguments at me. So in real life, it's just not a split. I have no problem with real-life people. Of course, on both sides of the Atlantic, I make a distinction between people I think are doing first-rate work and people I think are phonies. And I'm sure that all types of philosophy have their fair share.

There *are* some interesting differences in styles of philosophy, but they cut across the analytic-Continental divide. I think there is a very important difference among philosophers in how you regard the history of philosophy. And I think most of the people that I see as analytic philosophers feel that the history of the subject is a kind of mine where you can dig out ideas, but it does not constrain you; whereas I think most of the people who are so-called Continental philosophers, or at least a high percentage of them, are more Hegelian; they think that anything you do can only be understood in a historical and indeed a historicist fashion. And so they think that it's just *impossible* to do philosophy without this historical bent. I will give you one example of this: When I first started working on consciousness, my friend Jürgen Habermas was upset, he said, "No, no, no, go back to speech acts, stay with speech acts!" And it suddenly occurred to me, when he hears the word "consciousness," he thinks Hegel and thinks *Bewusstseinsphilosophie*. That is the last thing that would occur to me because I don't worry about the history of philosophy when I work on consciousness. When I hear "consciousness," I think "thalamocortical system," "massive synchronized rates of neuron firings," and I think of what it feels like. That is, I don't think in a historicist fashion, I don't think that in order to talk about consciousness you can only continue the chain of previous philosophical writings about consciousness—I am not interested in that. And that seems to me a really big difference among kinds of philosophers: how you regard the history of the subject.

Another big difference is how you regard science. Of course, the word "science" itself doesn't matter here, but how you regard intellectual results in subjects that are not philosophy, and there I think so-called analytic philosophers really want to make use of the results of science. I'll give you another example of this: Hannah Arendt wrote a book called *The Life of the Mind*. Now the fascinating thing is, for *her* the life of the mind is the history of philosophy. If I was going to write a book about the life of the mind, I would have to say a whole lot about quantum mechanics and relativity theory and Gödel's theorem—she says nothing about any of that. And I would have to say a lot about modernism in literature, about for example Proust, Joyce, Mann, and Kafka. I don't find anything about *them* in her book. For her, the life of the mind is the history of philosophy. And that really seems to me a big difference in kinds of philosophers—between those who think that the philosophy they do is a branch of the history of philosophy, and they are continuing this history and commenting on the history, and those who see it as a set of problems. And of course if you see it as a set of problems, then you get your problems and your methods from different sources. That for me is a much bigger difference than so-called Continental and analytic.

HRP: It's interesting that you talk about modernism and literature—I tend to think that the biggest division among philosophers is between those who concentrate on making use of science, versus those who focus on making use of literature, art, anthropology, and such fields. Is it true at all that you think science is more basic than those fields?

Searle: No, you see, I don't actually believe that it is useful to use the word "science." Science here, as we are using it now, is the name of a bunch of academic departments and disciplines—there is a sociological phenomenon called science, and it has a structure with jobs, and budgets, and research labs, and so on. What I am interested in is the results, the knowledge—the knowledge is everybody's property. The standard mistake in philosophy is to suppose that there is a branch of reality called "scientific reality"—that is what I am rejecting. There is *just* the real world. It happens that we know more about the real world than the Greeks did, and we have that knowledge for historical reasons—we have it because from the seventeenth century on, we found a set of ways of investigating the world that we came to call science. But I'm not interested now in science as a sociological phenomenon and an enterprise, but with knowledge—and the knowledge that counts for us is the result of this particular enterprise.

HRP: So you wouldn't say that the knowledge we get from science is more basic than the knowledge we gain from other fields?

Searle: There is just basic knowledge. For example, mathematics gives us basic knowledge. It's just that, for the set of questions that worry me, there has been an intellectual revolution, because we understand the fundamental structure of the real world—we understand the atomic structure, we understand the chemical bond, we understand some facts about biological evolution. You'll notice I said all of that without saying the word "science." These are just facts like any other facts, and now we start our philosophical investigation by asking: Well how can it be that biological beasts such as us, who are the result of five billion years of evolution, can have consciousness, Intentionality, free will, society, deontology, speech acts, politics, and all the rest of it? *That's* the philosophical question that interests me. But that's at a particular stage in the history of intellectual life—if I had lived in the thirteenth century, I wouldn't be able to say that.

HRP: So you don't believe that the problems you are working on are universal?

Searle: They're universal in the sense that they are absolutely general questions about human existence in relation to the rest of existence. They're not historicist questions—you can't answer the questions that interest me about the mind by doing an historical study about how people think differently at different times and places. Now in a way that makes the kind of philosophy I do more fun, because it *is* absolutely universal: all human beings perform speech acts, all human societies have social structures, all human beings have consciousness, they all have Intentionality. But now if you get into these other things that I've been working on, you find that they are very historically situated, like politics. Political philosophy is *not* timeless in a way that the philosophy of mind I do is timeless.

HRP: But you don't think that the way you are posing those general questions is somehow founded on basic presuppositions that we get from our culture?

Searle: Well of course everything we say is based on stuff we get from our culture, but that doesn't somehow make it less universally applicable. The fact that we have this knowledge which is now universal, established, and objective—we have overwhelming evidence about how the world is structured—enables us to proceed to investigate questions that we could not have investigated previously. But that does not cast any doubt at all on the universality of the investigation.

HRP: What about our knowledge of human reality? Do you think that there is a universal human nature?

Searle: I do, yes. We all have a common biological human nature that distinguishes us from dogs, cats, elephants, and even other primates. We are biological beasts, and what we call culture is the way in which different societies shape the underlying biological potential. But all human societies contain conscious beings, they all engage in Intentional behavior, they all perform speech acts, they all have social structures with various types of rights, duties, obligations, *et cetera*. Those phenomena are universal.

HRP: So the part of the background that's dependent on our culture isn't very important....

Searle: It is important for the investigation, because without the right sort of cultural background we would not know how to investigate things. But the subject matter of the investigation can go far beyond the background capacities that make the investigation possible. I live in a culture that makes my research possible, but that culture is not by itself the object of my research. The mistake that the Nietzschians make is to think that any word that has a history can't be defined, and everything has a history. Well, some things have more of a history than others.

HRP: I think you said once that you actually ignore the history of philosophy. Is that helpful?

Searle: For the most part that is true, but you cannot ignore it entirely. I went to Oxford at a time when basically they didn't care about the history of the subject. We learned Descartes, Locke, Berkeley, and Hume, and Descartes was an honorary Englishman for these purposes. And if you did Greats—that was the Classics degree at Oxford—you learned Plato and Aristotle. But I didn't know Greek, so I was told: don't bother to try to read Greek philosophy. (You should never tell undergraduates not to work—that's advice they take too eagerly.) So I am largely ignorant of—

I won't say largely, but I am pretty much ignorant of—large areas of the history of philosophy. Would I be a better philosopher if I spent more time on it? I don't know. I'm just not sure how it would have affected me. But certainly when I'm writing about the mind, I don't look back and wonder what Spinoza said or try to remind myself of what Descartes said about this—it never would occur to me. I mean a lot of people think you can't talk about Intentionality unless you first go back and do the history starting with the Greeks and the Medievals—I think that's a big mistake, then you're always stuck in that quagmire.... For the most part the problems of the great historical figures are not my problems. I can see that with some of them there is a continuity, but even in those cases—like the mind-body problem—the problem has been transformed in the three hundred and fifty years since Descartes wrote. So the history of philosophy is fun, but it's not what I do; it doesn't provide me with inspiration and it doesn't provide me with raw materials.

HRP: Do you think you have an intellectual debt to your education—do you think you've picked out your style of philosophy from early mentors?

Searle: I'm just not sure. The irony is: all of my philosophical education, except a very few courses at the University of Wisconsin—all of it came from Oxford. Now, when I go and lecture in England, people tell me I am a "typical American philosopher". And the people who taught me and inspired me were Peter Strawson and John Austin. They were the people who taught me how to do the subject. But I suppose my style may be— probably is—different from theirs. So if I'm asked how I learned how to do philosophy, well of course we are always self-taught. But the people who tried to teach me were Peter and Austin. And I learned more from them than I did from any of my other teachers. But, how much of my style is like theirs? I think Austin would feel...well Austin always used to say to me: "you're going *much* too fast" [with dramatic, British accent, and laughs]—and I think he probably would feel that to this day.

FUTURE PROJECTS

HRP: Do you have particular plans for the future? What's on your mind to work on this semester or next year?

Searle: Well, as I said, there is this continuing project that I was working on for years before I knew I was working on it, namely: How do you reconcile the human reality with the basic reality? Now you'd be surprised how few philosophers can hear that. I mean, one of my colleagues says, "Oh, that must be dualism, you must be a dualist." I said, I've spent all my life *militating against* dualism. But in any case, that's the question. Now, what forms does it take? The book that I would like to write, as I was mentioning earlier, is an extension of really two books—

The Construction of Social Reality and *Rationality in Action.* And it started out to extend those to the area of politics, but it keeps expanding, it keeps spilling over the side. So I would like to write a book about the ontology of civilization. I don't know if I can—that's a hard book to write.

Now another book that I have promised is an introductory book on the philosophy of mind. And at first I thought I did not want to do that. And then I thought, wait a second, I lecture on this, so I ought to be able to write a book on it. I have actually written a draft of that book. But the problem with that is that now having written a draft, it occurs to me that if this is going to be an introductory book, I should at least go read the other introductory books. So I have started reading them, and that's what I've been spending a lot of time doing. Because basically I don't read introductory text books, but now I'm reading a whole bunch of them on this subject and they all have this depressing feature that I mentioned earlier.

And then I'd kind of like to write a book in which I summarize the debates that I've had. Because people think of me as somehow pugnacious. (I don't think of myself that way at all. People say things that are false, I try to point out the error of their ways, I try to point out the mistakes, but I don't think of myself as especially argumentative. But maybe that just shows that self-analysis is a very poor method of self-knowledge, because a lot of people find me very pugnacious and argumentative.) Okay, but whether a good thing or bad, I have found myself in a whole lot of interesting arguments, and I thought: I'd like to write a book where I kind of summarize my arguments with my contemporaries. One, about artificial intelligence, one about higher education, one about my experiences with Oxford philosophy—these would be chapters of a single book—and one with various kinds of Continental philosophers, so-called deconstructionists. So, I mean, that might be a fun book to do, and I've actually written several chapters for fun.

HRP: What about things like art and literature...and human values like beauty, aesthetics? Have you figured out how those fit in?

Searle: I wish I knew. I am a total *Augenmensch.* When I go to any new city, the first place I go to is the art museum. I live in art museums. But I *have* written one article about that painting [points to a painting on his wall]— *Las Meninas*—which I think is about the second or third best picture ever painted; I think it's a fabulous picture, the Velázquez. And I would like to write more about aesthetics, but I just don't understand it well enough....

HRP: I think it has to fit in somewhere; it needs to be part of the big picture.

Searle: Absolutely. It has to be part of a total philosophical account of human reality and it cannot be a trivial part. It can't be—as it is for most philosophers and most philosophy departments—just a kind of leftover, the junk left over.

HRP: How about being out here in California—has that affected your work?

Searle: I don't know. I think I would probably have done more work if I had lived in a place that was less beautiful and less agreeable. I am not sure that I want the world to know this, but the truth is, Berkeley is paradise on earth. It's the most wonderful place. It has nearly everything—the climate is great, it's got the ocean, it's near to great skiing, it is incredibly prosperous and beautiful, it has a remarkably intelligent population. I have a friend who works in Cody's [a local bookstore], and she said a guy came up to the counter and was belligerent and said to the three women at the cash registers behind the counter, "What do you women know about books?" And the woman said, "You're looking at three doctors—I'm a Ph.D, she's a Ph.D, and she's an M.D. Now what are your credentials?" And the funny thing is, in Berkeley that's not surprising. I have no problems discussing intellectual issues with my gardener or my house cleaner—I love that.

HRP: How does teaching figure into your professional priorities?

Searle: I love it. I think it is regarded as somehow not intellectually respectable if you like teaching undergraduates. I *love* teaching undergraduates, especially Berkeley undergraduates. Because, you see, when I go somewhere else I have to teach them how to be Berkeley undergraduates—I have to teach them to raise their hand in lecture and ask a question. Now the Germans are hard to teach that at first [chuckles]—they're just not used to that. But at the end of three months of teaching in Berlin, they were all Berkeley students. Berkeley students approach philosophical lectures with enthusiasm tempered by respectful skepticism. So I like teaching; I like teaching intelligent, motivated undergraduates, and that's what I get in Berkeley, and I like teaching where it's as much of a dialogue as I can make it.

HRP: Has that helped you in the past?

Searle: I have students who give me good arguments, who make good objections, and who understand my work better than a lot of the professionals do. Yes, of course, I learn a lot from my students. φ

Notes:

[1] Rawls, John, "John Rawls: For the Record," in *Philosophers in Conversation: Interviews from* The Harvard Review of Philosophy (New York: Routledge, 2002), 10.

[2] Searle, John, *Intentionality* (Cambridge: Cambridge University Press, 1983), 79.

[3] Eco, Umberto, "Umberto Eco: On Semiotics and Pragmatism," in *Philosophers in Conversation: Interviews from* The Harvard Review of Philosophy (New York: Routledge, 2002), 26.

About *The Harvard Review of Philosophy*
Founded in 1991, *The Harvard Review of Philosophy* is a journal of profes-sional philosophy available in hundreds of libraries and philosophy departments in the United States and around the world. Past issues have included work by or interviews with many of the major figures in contemporary thought, including Noam Chomsky, Sir Karl Popper, W. V. Quine, and John Rawls.

Submissions
We are currently accepting submissions for Volume XIII (Fall 2005) of *The Harvard Review of Philosophy*. The *Review* welcomes articles on any philosophical subject, as well as interviews, book reviews, and responses to articles appearing in our current issue. Submissions must be sent by January 15th, 2005, preferably as a Microsoft Word file attached to an email to *hrp@hcs.harvard.edu*. Submissions may also be mailed, as a hard copy accompanied by a file on disk, to:

The Harvard Review of Philosophy
c/o Philosophy Tutorial Office
Emerson Hall 303
Harvard University
Cambridge, MA 02138

Inquiries should be directed to the email or postal addresses above. More information about submissions can be found on our website, www.harvardphilosophy.com. The *Review* reserves the right to edit articles for clarity.

Subscriptions
Subscriptions to the *Review* cost $10 per year for individuals and $50 per year for institutions. Shipping is free in the United States and Canada and $2 ($7 for airmail) elsewhere. To subscribe, visit the Sub-scriptions section of our website or send a check, made payable to *"The Harvard Review of Philosophy,"* to the address above, along with a mailing address and the number of years for which you would like to subscribe. Back issues of the *Review* including and after Vol. VIII (2000) are also available for the same price. Subscription inquiries should likewise be directed to the addresses above.

The *Review* Online
Further information about the *Review*, including a complete and search-able text archive of all previous issues, is available at www.harvardphilosophy.com.